GOOD★SPORTS

BY GLENN STOUT

AGAINST ALL ODDS

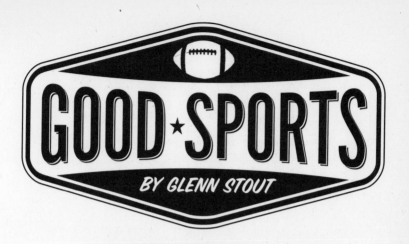

GOOD·SPORTS

BY GLENN STOUT

AGAINST ALL ODDS

sandpiper

HOUGHTON MIFFLIN HARCOURT
BOSTON NEW YORK 2012

For information about permission to reproduce selections from this book, write
to Permissions, Houghton Mifflin Harcourt Publishing Company, 215 Park
Avenue South, New York, New York 10003.

SANDPIPER and the SANDPIPER logo are trademarks of Houghton Mifflin
Harcourt Publishing Company.

www.hmhbooks.com

The text of this book is set in ITC Slimbach.

Jacket art © 2012: Frank Reich photo © Getty Images;
all other cover photos © Associated Press Images

Interior art © 2012 Associated Press Images

Library of Congress Cataloging-in-Publication Data
Stout, Glenn, 1958–.
Against all odds : never give up / by Glenn Stout.
p. cm. — (Good sports)
ISBN 978-0-547-88734-0
1. Sports—Psychological aspects. 2. Teamwork (Sports)—Psychological
aspects. 3. Success. I. Title.
GV706.55.S78 2012
796.01—dc23
2012023942

Manufactured USA
DOC 10 9 8 7 6 5 4 3 2 1
450037631

*This book is dedicated to everyone
who refuses to give up and keeps trying.*

CONTENTS

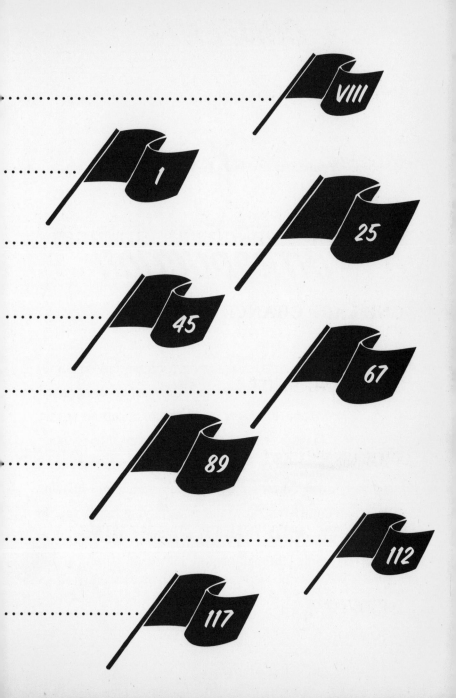

INTRODUCTION

QUITTING IS EASY.

Everyone who has ever played a sport has fallen behind, or lost, or made a terrible mistake that cost his or her team a victory. *No one,* not even an All-Star or an All-American, is perfect. Making errors and losing are part of the game.

However, whether one loses or makes a mistake isn't what is most important. What really matters is playing hard, giving it your best, and never giving up. If you do all that, you will win something even more important than any one game: the self-respect that comes from knowing you gave your best effort. That is the true goal of all sports.

The athletes and teams profiled in *Against All Odds: Never Give Up* either fell far, far behind or made a terrible mistake that cost their team a victory. But none of them ever quit or gave up. They kept playing the game with passion and integrity. In the end, they not only won on the field, but they also won something larger by setting a good example for others, by showing the right way to play.

So the next time you make a big mistake during a game, don't think about quitting: think about the way Roy Riegels, who almost ran for a touchdown in the wrong direction, was able to overcome his error. The next time your team falls far behind, don't try to win the game back all at once, but like basketball player Tracy McGrady or quarterback Frank Reich, just keep trying and doing your best, one play at a time. And when victory looks impossible, as it did for the St. Louis Cardinals in 2011, or Denver Broncos quarterback Tim Tebow, remember that if you never give up, you can still beat the odds and end up a winner.

Besides, *nothing* feels better than a comeback—doing what everyone else thinks can't be done!

Tim Tebow celebrates another amazing comeback victory.

THE COMEBACK KID

THE DENVER BRONCOS WERE FINISHED, and so too, it seemed, was the career of the backup quarterback Tim Tebow. Five games into the 2011 NFL season, as the Broncos faced AFC western division rival the San Diego Chargers, the Broncos were a dismal 1–4. Reaching the playoffs seemed virtually impossible. No team in NFL history had ever started the season 1–5 and then made the playoffs.

Tim Tebow was all but forgotten. Despite winning the Heisman Trophy as the best player in college football in 2007 and being selected in the first round by the Broncos in the 2010 NFL draft, thus far Tim Tebow had been a disappointment in the pros. As a rookie in 2010 he had played only sparingly and not impressed anyone, passing erratically and appearing overwhelmed. Before the start of the 2011 season, the Denver coach John Fox announced that Kyle Orton would be the team's number one quarterback and that Tim Tebow would serve as his backup.

During training camp and practice during the first month of the season, Tim was almost an afterthought. He didn't take a single snap with the first-team offense. Instead, Tim played for the scout team, imitating Denver's opponents against the Broncos' first-team defense. Thus far in the 2011 season Tim had appeared on the field for two plays, and those came during the Broncos' 49–23 loss to Green Bay. Although some Denver fans pleaded with the team to give Tebow a chance, most fans and sportswriters were beginning to consider Tim Tebow a wasted draft pick.

In the first half against San Diego, the Broncos continued to struggle. The Broncos' offense, in particular, had trouble moving the football, and as the two teams retreated to their locker rooms at halftime, the Broncos trailed 23–10. Then Coach John Fox made a decision. He pulled starting quarterback Kyle Orton from the lineup and told Tim Tebow that he would start the second half at quarterback. The Broncos had nothing to lose.

Tim tried to stay calm. "I was just very thankful for the

opportunity and wanted to make the most of it," he said later.

That he did. Although it took a while for him to get going, in the fourth quarter Tim led the team on two touchdown drives, running for one score and passing for another. Unfortunately, with the Broncos still trailing and driving downfield once again, they ran out of time as Tim's desperation pass fell incomplete on the final play of the game.

"It never feels good losing," said Tebow at a press conference after the game. "It definitely puts a bad taste in your mouth. We just have to go out there and work and get better, so hopefully we don't have to feel that way this often again." Although the loss dropped the Broncos' record to 1–5, Tim Tebow was not prepared to give up on the season.

Over the next few months the rest of the NFL would learn just how badly Tim and his teammates wanted to get rid of that bad taste and taste victory instead.

Tim Tebow was just getting started.

Another player may well have been ready to give up, but Tim Tebow wasn't just another football player. He had been beating the odds and doing things that others thought were impossible ever since he was a young boy. Tim Tebow believed in himself. And just because he was a backup quarterback did not mean that Tim had stopped believing. He knew that all he needed was a chance.

The odds had been against Tim from before he was born. His father, Robert, was a pastor in the Baptist Church, and he and his wife, Pamela, were serving as missionaries in the Philippines when Pam learned she was pregnant. Before Tim was born she became ill, and doctors did not expect her baby, the Tebows' fifth child, to survive birth. They were shocked when Tim was born healthy and strong.

The Tebows eventually returned to the United States, and Tim was raised in Jacksonville, Florida. Tim's older brothers loved sports, and when Tim was a young boy he tried to follow in their footsteps. Like his brothers, Tim played baseball, basketball, and football in local youth leagues. Tall and strong and fast, Tim was one of the best young players in the area. Football was his favorite sport, and he dreamed of playing quarterback in high school.

The Tebows, who are very religious, chose to home-school their children, teaching them at home so they could provide both academic and religious instruction. As a result, for a while it seemed as if Tim wouldn't have the same opportunities to play sports as children who attended public or private schools.

Fortunately, in 1996 the state of Florida passed a law that allowed homeschooled children to play sports for their local schools. Tim's brother Peter first took advantage of the law and earned all-state honors in both football and baseball, and earned a college football scholarship as a linebacker. When Tim was old enough for high school, he began playing for local school teams as well, first playing tight end and linebacker at nearby Trinity Christian Academy.

Tim, however, really wanted to play quarterback. Unfortunately, Trinity's offense was based on running the football and Tim had no opportunity to play quarterback and throw the ball. After one year Tim decided to play football for nearby Nease High School, where Coach Craig Howard was installing a wide-open, pass-oriented offense.

Although some people didn't think that a homeschooled athlete had enough experience to succeed at a big high school like Nease, particularly someone like Tim, who hadn't played quarterback in his first year of high school, Tim proved everyone wrong. Standing six foot three and weighing 225 pounds, Tim soon became the Panthers' starting quarterback. Not only did Tim have a strong arm, but he was a rugged runner. With Tim at quarterback, the Nease Panthers became one of the best teams in the state of Florida. Tim became recognized as one of the best quarterbacks in high school football. Dozens and dozens of colleges approached Tim with offers of scholarships. He eventually decided to attend the University of Florida.

The Gators' offense was perfect for a player like Tim, who could both run and pass the ball. As a freshman he was a backup to starter Chris Leak, but under Coach Urban Meyer, Tim still received the opportunity to play. Meyer occasionally sent him into the game to take advantage of his running ability. Tim ended the season as the team's second best rusher.

He became the starting quarterback in 2007. Although some questioned his skills as a passer, Tim proved them wrong, winning the Heisman Trophy as the best college football player in America. His success continued in 2008 and 2009, as he led the Gators to a national championship in 2008 and to a 13–1 record in 2009. Moreover, he won the respect of his teammates, who twice named him team captain.

Yet despite his record of leadership and his performance, people were not convinced that Tim could be a starting quarterback in the NFL. Professional football is much more complex than the college game, particularly on pass plays. A quarterback must learn to read the defense almost instantaneously and decide which receiver will be open. Defenders are much faster and bigger, and quarterbacks have to release the ball quickly and throw more accurately than in college. Many star college quarterbacks discover they simply can't cut it in the NFL.

Many pro scouts looked at Tim and didn't see a successful pro quarterback. At Florida Tim ran an "option" offense, meaning that on almost every play he had to decide whether to run the ball himself or give it to a running back. Since opponents had to be ready for the run, when he passed, his receivers were usually wide open. Although Florida's offense had been perfect for Tim's set of skills, it had not prepared him for pro football, and Tim developed some bad habits, such as holding the ball low and winding up before he threw rather than releasing the pass quickly.

Although some observers, such as former NFL coach Jon Gruden, thought Tim could succeed and with his size and strength he would "revolutionize" the quarterback position, most agreed with the respected analyst Mel Kiper, who stated bluntly, "I don't think he can be a full-time quarterback." Most expected Tim to be picked in the third or fourth round of the draft. Some even thought he might go undrafted, or be asked by his team to change positions in pro football and become either a running back or tight end.

However, Denver's coach at the time, Josh McDaniels, believed in Tim. Although he admitted that he didn't expect Tim to start as a rookie, McDaniels loved Tebow's leadership skills and said, "He has all the traits you look for." Tim was thrilled to be selected by the Broncos and told a reporter, "My greatest joy in Denver is going to be to repay Coach McDaniels for believing in me." Still, it was a risky pick. Many people thought that by picking Tim in the first round, McDaniels had put his job on the line. If Tim failed, McDaniels could lose his job.

That's exactly what happened. Near the end of the 2010 season, with a record of 3–9, McDaniels was fired. Although drafting Tim Tebow was not the only reason he was let go, it didn't help.

After nearly leading the Broncos to a comeback victory over the Chargers in the sixth game of the 2011 season for the new coach, John Fox, Fox named Tim the starting quarterback for the Broncos' next game, against the Miami Dolphins.

Although some Denver fans were thrilled, many thought that by electing to play Tim, the Broncos were giving up on the season. There were several talented quarterbacks who would become eligible for the draft after the season, and some thought the Broncos were hoping to lose so they could get a low draft pick and draft a new quarterback. They still thought Tim didn't have the skills to succeed in the NFL.

For the first fifty-five minutes of the game against the Dolphins, Tim's critics seemed to be correct. He was terrible. As the *New York Times* noted later, he "barely looked like a functioning NFL quarterback. . . . He took sacks and threw poorly. He was hesitant and overwhelmed." Tim completed only three of eight passes for twenty-four yards as the Dolphin led 15–0. The situation looked hopeless. Yet as everyone would soon learn, Tim Tebow never gives up.

The Broncos took over with just over five minutes remaining. Suddenly, Tim came alive, throwing the ball accurately and with authority. He marched the team down the field, and then, with the ball at the eighteen-yard line, Tim dropped back to pass.

All his receivers were covered. Earlier in the game he might have forced a throw or, with the defensive line closing in on him, taken a sack.

This time, however, Tim went to his strength. He retreated more than ten yards, avoiding tacklers, then abruptly changed direction and headed upfield. He cut toward the sideline, forcing one defender to miss by making a 360-degree spin move before being forced out of bounds at the five-yard line. One play later, he hit receiver Demaryius Thomas in the end zone for a touchdown. Still, the Broncos were running out of time. After the extra point made the score 15–7, the Broncos kicked off. But instead of booting the ball downfield, they tried and recovered an on-side kick to get the back near midfield.

Tim once again drove the Broncos down the field. On first down from the three-yard line, he rolled out. All his receivers appeared to be covered.

All but one, that is. Tim, thinking fast, realized that tight end Daniel Fells, his "safety valve," was wide open. Tim turned and calmly floated a pass his direction, and Fells rumbled into the end zone to make the score 15–13. In order to tie the game, the Broncos had to go for a two-point conversion.

They turned to Tim. He took the snap and powered his

way into the end zone to tie the game. The contest entered overtime, and a few moments later Denver kicker Matt Prater kicked a long field goal to win the game. The Broncos became the first team in more than forty years to come back and win after trailing by fifteen points or more with only three minutes remaining in the game.

"We were able to make that play this week and we believed," said Tim after the game. "I know I keep saying that, but I don't know how many times it was said to me, and I said it to other guys throughout the game. I think that was, at least what I took away, the biggest thing of the game."

The next week, however, Tim and the Broncos came crashing down to earth. After the Broncos had taken a 3–0 lead against the playoff-bound Detroit Lions, the Lions scored forty-five unanswered points as Tim struggled en route to a 45–10 defeat. On nine of fifteen possessions, Tim failed to lead the Broncos to a first down.

After the game, his critics came out in force. One called his playing "one of the worst performances in the history of quarterbacking." Once again people were saying he didn't have the skills to play quarterback in the NFL. As another wrote, "Sure, he's a nice guy, but just because you're a good guy doesn't mean you're going to succeed in the NFL."

All over the country, on talk radio and online, fans and

sports writers criticized and made fun of Tim. Once again, it would have been easy for him to quit, but that's not who Tim Tebow is. As he later said, he didn't listen to the criticism: "I've said this before, but I never thought I was a finished product. I never said I was. I never believed I was. I'm going to work every day as hard as I can, one game at a time, one day at a time. . . . I just put that pressure on myself more than anybody else to try to get better and to try to improve." Besides, Tim's coaches and his teammates still believed in him. As Broncos linebacker Von Miller said later, "Tim Tebow? I'm buying. He's the greatest thing out there." Denver tackle Orlando Franklin agreed, saying, "All the fans know it, his teammates know it: He brings a little bit more to the huddle."

A week later, against the Oakland Raiders, Tim did just that. Despite trailing at halftime, Tim led the Broncos to thirty second-half points and a 38–24 victory. It helped that the Broncos installed a new offense, a run-oriented strategy known as the "read option" similar to the offense Tim had run at the University of Florida. Tim felt much more comfortable, and it showed.

But once again, the critics came out in force. No other team in the NFL was using such an offense. They were certain that in the long run, Tim and the new offense would fail.

Instead, the opposite happened. As Tim and his teammates grew more accustomed to the offense, the Broncos kept getting better. Although they often fell behind early, at the end of the game Tim and his teammates somehow figured out a way to win.

After beating the Kansas City Chiefs 17–10, the Broncos faced the New York Jets, a team some people expected to make it to the Super Bowl.

Once again, Tim struggled early. Trailing 13–10 with a little more than five minutes remaining, the game all but over, the Broncos got the ball at the five-yard line. So far, the Jets defense had shut Tim and the Broncos down, holding the team to just over one hundred yards in the first fifty-five minutes of the game. Now Tim had only five minutes to move the ball ninety-five yards downfield.

All of a sudden, he was on fire and pushed the ball downfield. On third down at the twenty-yard line, with just over a minute remaining, Tim took the snap from center and dropped back to pass.

The Jets blitzed. Tim retreated quickly, moving another ten yards back to avoid a sack.

Looking downfield, he saw that all his receivers were covered. But he also saw that the left side of the field was wide open.

He sprinted to his left, outrunning a rusher, broke into the clear, and turned upfield. The startled Jets tried to react, but Tim was too fast and too strong. At the ten-yard line a defender dove at Tim from behind. He stumbled, but stayed upright and charged into the end zone.

"Touchdown!" The crowd at Denver's Mile High Stadium went crazy as Tim was surrounded by his teammates and he bent to one knee to give a silent prayer. Meanwhile, as the clock ran down and the Broncos won, 17–13, the Jets looked on, shaking their heads as if unable to believe what had just happened. Tim Tebow had done it again! "You want opportunities like this," he said after the game, "because this is an opportunity for greatness."

Finally it seemed as if Tim's critics were beginning to believe in him the same way his fans and teammates did. As the sportswriter Mike Klis of the *Denver Post* wrote, "All the critics are right when they say Tebow can't pass accurately, can't read defenses all that well, can't operate a conventional offense. And in the end, all the critics are wrong. Tebow is magical. Tebow is a winner. Tebow is the one and only." All of a sudden, with a record of 5–5, the Broncos were in position to make a run to the playoffs.

The impossible and the improbable suddenly seemed to become normal for Tim and the Broncos. In their next game against the Chargers, Tim led the team to another late drive that resulted in a game-tying field goal. The Broncos won with another field goal in overtime to make the score 16–13. Although Tim played a key role in the victory, he characteristically gave his teammates credit. "I'm just having fun and surrounded by a great bunch of guys and great coaches," he said. "We're just believing, and it's such a positive atmosphere. . . . It's a special team when you got a bunch of guys that when things aren't going good, we get closer instead of pulling apart. . . . I think that's really special and I think that's hard to find. I think the number one reason we're like that is because we believe in each other and believe in the coaching staff."

One week later, against the Minnesota Vikings, Tim gave his teammates and their fans more reasons to believe. With the team trailing 15–10 at halftime, Tim led the Broncos to twenty-eight second-half points, throwing for two touchdowns and scoring on a two-point conversion as the Broncos won 35–32 on Matt Prater's field goal. Then, in their next game against the Chicago Bears, the Broncos did it again.

Trailing 10–0 with only a little over four and a half minutes remaining in the game, Tim led the Broncos down the field and threw a touchdown pass to make the score 10–7. "Tim came in [the huddle] and just talked to us," said receiver Demaryius Thomas after the game. "He just said, 'Get first down after first down.' We did that and got more chances and more chances." A moment later, Denver got the ball back, Tim completed three passes, and Matt Prater connected on a fifty-nine-yard field goal to send the game into overtime, where Prater, after Tim led the Broncos downfield again, hit another field goal to win the game. With Tim Tebow at quarterback, comebacks were becoming commonplace.

Less than two months earlier, Tim Tebow had been sitting on the bench and the Broncos were going nowhere. Now they were 8-5 and Tim Tebow's name was on the lips of every football fan in America. No player in pro football history had led his team to so many amazing comebacks in one season. But Tim still had one more comeback, one even more amazing, left to accomplish.

When the Broncos had installed their new offense, it had surprised opponents, but toward the end of the season they began to adapt. After winning six games in a row, Tim and the Broncos lost their last three contests to the New England Patriots, the Buffalo Bills, and the Kansas City Chiefs. And in those final three games, Tim hadn't played very well, and the offense in particular had struggled. Nevertheless, the Broncos still qualified for the playoffs and faced the Pittsburgh Steelers in the first round.

In the days before the playoff contest, Tim's critics again came out in force. Some argued that he had been successful only because of the Broncos' offense, and because the Broncos had played a weak schedule, with most of their success during the winning streak coming against poor teams. Others thought he was lucky, and some chose to make fun of him for the way he gave credit to his teammates and expressed his religious faith on the field by pointing to the sky or bowing down on one knee to pray after each victory.

If the criticism bothered Tim, he didn't show it. He was unapologetic in regard to his religious views and optimistic over his team's chances in the playoffs. "It's win or go home," said Tim before the game. Even his detractors knew that Tim intended to do all he could to help his team win.

Still, few people outside the Broncos locker room gave Denver much of a chance against the Steelers. Not only was quarterback Ben Roethlisberger one of the best quarterbacks in the NFL, but the Steelers defense, known as the "Steel Curtain," had given up the fewest points in the league.

Mile High Stadium was full when the game began, with most Broncos fans already screaming themselves hoarse and decked out in the Broncos colors, blue and orange. Soon, however, the cheering stopped.

Pittsburgh dominated the first quarter. The Broncos managed to run only seven plays and gain eight yards, as Tim missed several wide-open receivers. Meanwhile, even though the Broncos had kept the Steelers out of the end zone, Pittsburgh was moving the ball up and down the field and led 6–0 on two field goals. Against a team like the Steelers, the Broncos could not afford to fall behind.

Then things got even worse. On the first play of the second quarter, with Denver facing a second-down-and-twelve-yards-to-go situation on their eighteen-yard line. Tim threw a pass to wide receiver Eric Decker. He appeared to make a great catch before being tackled by the Steelers' star linebacker James Harrison, but the Steelers challenged the call and the catch was overturned. Even worse, Decker was hurt on the play and knocked from the game. Tim and the Broncos would have to play without their leading receiver. But if Tim and the Broncos had proven anything over the course of the 2011 season, it was that they were the most dangerous when things looked hopeless.

On the next play Tim dropped back and looked downfield. He quickly scanned his receivers, looking for a man open, but the Steelers had everyone covered.

As Tim began to feel the pass rush, he started to scramble and his receivers broke from their planned pass routes and just tried to get open. Tim saw Demaryius Thomas streaking down the left sideline and threw a bomb.

The pass was perfect as Thomas ran under the ball for a fifty-one-yard completion. One play later, Tim found receiver Eddie Royal down the right sideline. Unfortunately, the Pittsburgh defender had him well covered.

Tim threw the ball anyway. As Royal turned for the ball in the end zone it dropped perfectly into his hands, just over the defender's outstretched arm. Touchdown, Denver!

It was the Broncos' first touchdown in their last twenty-one possessions. The play gave Tim and his teammates confidence, and the Denver coaches began to realize that the Steelers didn't really respect the Broncos' passing attack and believed all the critics who said Tim couldn't throw. As a result, the Steelers' defensive backs were looking for the run.

The Broncos decided to keep throwing long, a strategy they had hardly used during the regular season. It was up to Tim to put the strategy into effect.

Denver stopped the Steelers and got the ball back. Tim dropped back to pass once again. This time he spotted Demaryius Thomas wide open in the middle of the field. Thomas pulled the pass in and weaved his way forward for a fifty-eight-yard gain.

Then Tim took over. With the ball on the eight-yard line he took the snap and burst up the middle, plowing over star defensive back Troy Polamalu for a touchdown.

Although Pittsburgh managed to keep the Broncos out of the end zone in their next two drives, Tim still put the Broncos in field goal range twice more, and at halftime Denver led 20–6. The Steelers were stunned.

During halftime, as the players rested, Tim, Demaryius Thomas, and the Broncos coaching staff discussed Pittsburgh's defense. They had all noticed the way Pittsburgh's safeties were creeping toward the line of scrimmage, leaving them vulnerable to a long pass over the top. To take advantage, they designed a new play that called for Tim to fake a handoff to a running back and then throw the ball to Thomas. Although they had never even practiced the play before, under the right situation they thought it could go for a touchdown — if Tim could make the throw.

In the second half the Steelers showed why they had been heavily favored to win. They stormed back to tie the game 23–23. Although each team had a chance to go ahead in the final minutes, neither team could manage to score.

The game entered overtime. Captains of both teams gathered at midfield for the coin toss. The Steelers called tails, but the coin landed heads up and the Broncos elected to receive the kick. After the Pittsburgh kicker booted the ball deep into the end zone, the Broncos took over on the twenty-yard line.

Broncos offensive coordinator Mike McCoy had already told Tim and Demaryius Thomas that they would use the new play if they won the toss. The two players entered the huddle knowing what would happen next as Tim called the play.

The Broncos lined up in the same formation they usually used on a running play. The Steelers recognized that and their defensive backs started to cheat toward the line of scrimmage.

Tim stood behind the line in "shotgun" position and barked out the signals as Demaryius Thomas set up wide to the left, the only wide receiver. Then center J. D. Walton snapped Tim the ball.

Tim grabbed the ball from the air and turned to his left as running back Willis McGahee approached and opened his arms as if to receive the handoff. Thomas broke down-field. The Steelers were so certain the Broncos were going to run the ball that every defender but one was within five yards of the line of scrimmage.

Thomas angled toward the center of the field, putting space between himself and the cornerback. Tim raised his arm to pass the ball. Pittsburgh's defensive backs put on the brakes and scrambled to get back in position.

Ten yards downfield, Thomas beat his man to the inside. Tim saw that he was open and fired the ball.

The pass was perfect. Thomas caught it on the dead run and saw an open field in front of him.

Pittsburgh's cornerback reached out to try to stop him, but Thomas put out his arm, pushed him away, and sprinted toward the end zone. Each step drew him closer to victory. As the Denver crowd stood on their feet and roared, Tim and his teammates started racing upfield after Thomas.

Ten yards from the end zone, another Pittsburgh player dove for Thomas's feet. He missed, and when the receiver crossed into the end zone, the Broncos were winners, 29–23. With an eighty-yard touchdown pass, the longest scoring play in NFL overtime playoff history, Tim Tebow had led his teammates to yet another amazing comeback! He finished the game with ten completions in twenty-one passes for a career-high 316 yards, 204 of them on four catches by Thomas.

After the game, however, Tim refused to take personal credit for the victory. "I just tried to fit it in there, and he made a great catch. . . . They came out and they played hard and we played hard, and it was a great game, and I'm very thankful we were able to get the win."

Tim and his teammates were already looking ahead to the next game. If they kept believing in each other there was no way of telling what would happen next.

Unfortunately for Tim and the Broncos, in the next round of the playoffs there would be no comeback as they were defeated by the New England Patriots. When star quarterback Peyton Manning of the Indianapolis Colts became available in the off-season, the Broncos signed him to a contract and traded Tim Tebow to the New York Jets.

Roy Riegels holds his head after making a sixty-four-yard run in the wrong direction in the 1929 Rose Bowl.

MAKING A WRONG TURN OUT RIGHT

IMAGINE MAKING A HUGE MISTAKE in the biggest game of your life in front of thousands and thousands of people.

Now imagine that your mistake not only cost your team a victory, but gave you a humiliating nickname people would remember for the rest of your life. How would you come back from that?

Would you feel like a loser, run off the field, and quit the team, too embarrassed to continue? Or would you strive to overcome your mistake?

That was the choice that confronted Roy Riegels. In the biggest game of his career he made perhaps the most memorable mistake in the history of football. But instead of making excuses, Roy admitted his error. Instead of quitting, he became determined to succeed. And because he did, he was seen not as a goat who cost his team a win, but as a person of character and integrity.

Roy Riegels made a huge mistake, but he did not let that error define who he was. The way he responded proved to everyone that he was not a loser. In the end, he won a victory greater than that of any football game.

Roy Riegels grew up in Oakland, California, and enrolled at the University of California in nearby Berkeley. In his sophomore year in 1927 he joined the varsity football team, coached by Clarence "Nibs" Price.

Roy Riegels was one of Price's best players. Standing six feet tall and weighing about 170 pounds, Roy was smart, rugged, and strong.

In the 1920s football was played much differently than it is today. Players wore leather helmets without face masks. The football was rounder, and the center often snapped the ball not to the quarterback, but to a halfback. Few teams passed the ball more than a handful of times each game.

Rules prevented teams from making many substitutions, so most players in college football played both offense and defense, often staying on the field for the entire game. When the California Golden Bears were on offense, Roy Riegels played center, snapping the ball to one of the backs to start every play and then blocking. On defense, he played a position then known as center, similar to what today is called a middle linebacker, a key position on the defense. Before each play Roy would crouch opposite the center of the opposing team and check to make sure his teammates were in position. When the ball was snapped he would have to fend off blockers and try to make a tackle. Considered one of the leaders of the Golden Bears defense, Roy ranged all over the field, stopping both runs up the middle and chasing down ball carriers when they tried to run around the end.

Roy played both positions to near perfection, and the Golden Bears improved from a 3–6 finish the previous year to end the season 7–3. Based on that performance, at the start of the 1928 season the Golden Bears were expected to challenge the mighty Trojans of the University of Southern California for the Pacific Coast Conference championship.

Led by Riegels and talented halfback Benny Lom, the Golden Bears played hard all season long. Although they sometimes had trouble scoring against tougher opponents, Roy anchored one of the best defenses in the country. In nine regular-season games, the Bears gave up only thirty-four points. They lost only once — to the Olympic Athletic Club, a semiprofessional team from San Francisco that included players much older and more experienced than the Golden Bears. On two occasions the Golden Bears tied their opponent, playing the USC Trojans to a scoreless standoff and tying the Stanford Cardinals, 13–13. Riegels played a key role in that game, as his block helped spring teammate Steve Bancroft for a seventy-five-yard touchdown run. The Bears finished the Pacific Coast Conference season with a record of three wins, no losses, and two ties, second to USC, which finished 4–0–1 and was ranked number one in the country. Riegel's teammates showed how much respect they had for him by electing him team captain for the up-coming season.

In the 1920s, professional football was just getting started and did not have a very big following. College football, on the other hand, was extremely popular. The biggest game of the season and the last game of the year was the Rose Bowl, the only postseason game at the time. Known today as "the granddaddy of them all" because it inspired dozens of other postseason bowl games, the Rose Bowl was first played in 1902 and often matched up the two best teams in college football. In 1923 organizers built a new stadium, also called the Rose Bowl, for the game. At the time it was the largest stadium in the country, capable of holding more than fifty thousand fans. It was eventually expanded to a capacity of more than one hundred thousand.

Played on New Year's Day in Pasadena, California, the Rose Bowl was as big as the Super Bowl is today. Football fans everywhere looked forward to it. The week before the game sportswriters from all over the country gathered in Pasadena to interview players and coaches and write stories about the upcoming match. Fans traveled by train from all over the nation to see it. Those who could not make the trip looked forward to listening to the game on a nationwide radio broadcast.

Although Bowl officials usually asked the two best teams in the country to play, at the end of the 1928 season USC administrators decided not to allow the Trojans to appear in the game. As a result, Rose Bowl officials invited the second- and third-ranked teams in the country—the University of California Golden Bears and the Yellow Jackets of Georgia Tech. Each team accepted the invitation and started practicing for the big game. Most players realized it would probably be the biggest game of their football careers.

Roy and his teammates knew that Georgia Tech would give them a tough game. The Yellow Jackets had finished the 1928 season a perfect 9–0, outscoring their opponents 213–40. Led by running back Jack "Stumpy" Thomason, the Yellow Jackets featured a punishing running attack that often wore down their opponents.

One reason for that record was Riegel's counterpart on the Yellow Jackets, All-American center Peter Pund, one of the best players in the country. Standing six foot two and weighing two hundred pounds, Pund was considerably bigger than Riegel. Legendary football coach Knute Rockne of Notre Dame, whose team lost to Georgia Tech 13–0 in 1928, later said of Pund, "I counted twenty scoring plays that this man ruined. . . . We were hopelessly beaten — but I had the thrill of my life to see great fighters go down in defeat before a greater fighter." Pund led the Yellow Jackets defense and in 1969 was selected by the College Football Hall of Fame as the greatest center of the 1920s.

Riegels knew that defeating Pund and his Georgia Tech teammates would be difficult, but in the weeks before the game he and his fellow Bears were confident. They practiced hard and entered the game crisp and sharp. Although they knew the contest might be close, they still liked their chances against the Yellow Jackets.

It was sunny and warm in Pasadena on the day of the

game. More than sixty thousand football fans poured into the Rose Bowl, most expecting to see a defensive battle.

In the first period they were not disappointed. Depending primarily on the run, neither team had much success moving the ball. They traded punts several times and the first quarter ended with the score 0–0. In such a close game, players on both teams knew the outcome might depend on a single play.

Roy was playing well, but Peter Pund was giving him all he could handle. Sportswriters noted that Roy was taking a terrific pounding yet showed no signs of giving up.

Midway through the second quarter, with the game still scoreless, the Yellow Jackets received a punt and took over at their own twenty-four-yard line. On first down the Yellow Jackets quarterback took the snap from the center, spun around, and handed the ball to their squat running back, Stumpy Thomason.

Thomason wrapped the ball in his arms and took off toward left tackle. But the California line held its ground. With no room to run through the line, Thomason broke toward the left sideline.

From his position over the center, Riegels saw the Georgia Tech linemen blocking to the left and he started sliding down the line, fighting off blockers and following the play.

As Thomason bounced outside, Riegels began to sprint toward the sideline so he would be in position to make a tackle if Thomason made it around the end.

As Thomason reached the line of scrimmage, he shrugged off a California tackler, took a few strides toward the sideline, then turned straight upfield. He held the ball tightly under his left arm and raised his right arm to fend off tacklers.

At the twenty-eight-yard line a tackler appeared in front of Thomason, but the running back spun a full 360 degrees, leaving the California defender holding only air. Thomason then managed to sidestep another tackler only to find as he approached the thirty-yard line that he was about to be sandwiched between two more California defenders, back Benny Lom and end Irving Phillips. He put his head down and charged ahead.

One man grabbed him by the waist and the other climbed on his back, pinning his arms and pushing him toward the ground. As Thomason began to fall, Reigels, still running hard, was on track to intercept the running back just in case he managed to break free.

But as Thomason fell to the ground, his legs churning, he lost his grasp on the football. It popped out ahead of him, bouncing on the ground.

Although today's college rules don't allow defenders to run back fumbles, in 1929 that rule was not in effect. Any player on either team could pick up the ball and run with it. Roy Riegels was in the perfect position to recover the fumble.

When Roy saw the ball bouncing free he bent at his waist and scooped it up with both hands. Although he was accustomed to handling the ball while playing center, as a lineman Roy never had the opportunity to run with it. Yet all of a sudden the ball was in his hands. Without breaking stride he turned upfield.

Three quick strides took him past the pile where Thomason now lay sprawled on the ground. Then Roy saw a wall of Georgia Tech players racing his way. He veered to his left, looking for daylight and hoping to avoid being tackled. He wanted to make the most of his rare opportunity to carry the football.

As one tackler launched himself at Roy's feet, he nimbly skipped out of the way and then bumped into the referee. All of a sudden, Roy saw nothing but an open field ahead and heard nothing but the roar of the crowd. "I looked around, saw some goalposts, and made for them," he said later.

Roy started running as fast as he could. After only a few

strides he was in a full sprint. No player on either team was within five yards of him.

It was one of the most exciting moments of Roy's young life. In the biggest game of his career, Roy was sure he was going to score a touchdown and be the hero of the game.

There was just one small problem—actually, one BIG problem. When Roy had cut away from the tacklers and bumped into the referee, he had become disoriented and lost his sense of direction. Instead of running toward the California goal line, he was going in the opposite direction, toward Georgia Tech's end zone. Roy Riegels was running the wrong way!

For a second, everyone was confused, and a few of Roy's teammates even started to block for him. Then Benny Lom, back on his feet after tackling Thomason, saw Roy dash by with the ball and suddenly realized what was happening.

Lom knew he had to stop Roy and took off after him, as did the entire Georgia Tech team.

Meanwhile, Roy was running as fast as he could and by now had a good ten yards on Lom. "Stop! Stop!" Lom yelled out between breaths as he chased his teammate. "Turn back! You're going the wrong way!"

With the crowd roaring, Riegels could barely hear his teammate and didn't understand why Lom was yelling at him. In his confusion Roy thought Lom wanted him to give Lom the ball so Lom, and not Roy, could score the touchdown. As he ran he called out, "Get away from me! This is my touchdown!"

Roy just kept running, getting closer to the wrong end zone with each step.

In the press box, radio announcer Graham McNamee, like the other sixty-four thousand people in the stadium that day, could not believe what he was seeing. He had broadcast dozens of football games before but had never, ever seen a player run the wrong way. Huddled around their radios, fans listened in disbelief as they heard McNamee screaming as he watched Riegels sprint toward the Tech end zone. "What am I seeing?" he asked breathlessly. "Am I crazy? Am I crazy? Am I *crazy?*"

He was not crazy. Roy Riegels was still running the wrong way!

Roy was fast for a center, but Benny Lom was faster. At the ten-yard line, Lom finally caught up to his teammate. He reached out, grabbed the back of his jersey to slow him down, and started yelling again. *"You're going the wrong way. You're going the wrong way!"*

Suddenly Roy understood, and one of the greatest moments in his life instantly became one of the worst. He knew he had to try to turn around and run in the right direction, but his momentum carried him closer to the goal line.

By the time he could stop he was only a foot or two away from the end zone. He turned to run upfield but saw a sea of Georgia Tech tacklers only a few yards away, running full speed toward him. Roy started to run the right way, but before he took even a full step he disappeared in a swarm of Yellow Jackets and was knocked back into the end zone. As he lay on the ground beneath a pile of players, Roy wanted to dig a hole and hide. He could not believe what he had just done.

Fortunately for Roy and the Golden Bears, the referee marked the ball at the one-yard line. Instead of being tackled in the end zone for a safety, which would have given two points to Georgia Tech, the Golden Bears still had the ball and the game was still scoreless.

But that did not make Roy Riegels feel any better. As Roy huddled with his teammates the Yellow Jackets looked at him, smirking, while over sixty thousand fans laughed and roared at what had just happened. Roy knew that millions of people all over the country listening to the game on the radio were having a similar reaction.

He just wanted to disappear. The game was like a bad dream that wouldn't end.

But there was no time to hide in shame. Coach Price, afraid that if he called a running play, one of the California backs would be tackled in the end zone for a safety, decided to have Benny Lom punt on the next play. If Lom could kick the ball forty or fifty yards back downfield, and the Bears stopped the Yellow Jackets from scoring, perhaps no one would remember Roy Riegels ran the wrong way. Roy hoped that was true.

Lom took the snap, stepped forward, and kicked the ball, but the fired-up Yellow Jackets defense broke through on the left side of the line. A Georgia Tech player reached up and blocked the kick. The ball spun crazily on the ground and into the end zone, and then everyone dove for it. Fortunately, the Golden Bears recovered the ball and denied the Yellow Jackets a touchdown, but by downing the ball in the end zone, Georgia Tech still received a safety worth two points. California now trailed, 2–0. The two teams traded punts for the rest of the quarter and then both squads jogged off the field for halftime.

When he reached the locker room Roy covered his shoulders with a blanket, sat on a bench, put his head in his hands, and began to cry. His teammates tried to make him feel better, slapping him on the back and telling him it was okay. California fullback Jim Cockburn even tried to get Roy to smile. "What's the idea of running sixty-five yards on such a hot day," he asked, "when you only had to go thirty-five in the other direction?" But nothing anyone did or said took away the sting of embarrassment that Roy felt.

Before sending his team back out on the field, Coach Price gave the Bears a quick pep talk. He told them to forget about Riegels's run and just go out and play hard during the second half. Then he announced that the same players who started the first half would start the second half — and that included Roy. But as his teammates headed back out on the field, Roy stayed behind, sitting on the bench with his head in his hands.

When Price approached him, Roy began to speak. "Coach," he said, "I can't do it. I've ruined *you,* I've ruined *the school*. I've ruined *myself*. I couldn't face the crowd in that stadium to save my life." He was ready to quit.

Coach Price looked at the young man and spoke, his voice soft but strong. "Roy," he said. "Get up and go back." Then he added, "The game is only half over."

Roy looked at his coach and thought about his words for

a moment. At that instant he realized he had two choices. He could give up, quit, and allow one mistake to destroy his life, or else he could get up and go on. He did not know it at the time, but his decision would be perhaps the most important one of his life.

After a moment Roy took a deep breath, stood up, and tossed the blanket from his shoulders. Then he lifted his head and jogged back onto the field after his teammates.

He was not a loser. He was down, but he was not defeated. He was not going to quit and he was not going to give up. He would not let one mistake ruin his life, and if Roy could do anything about it, he was not going to let his mistake cost his team a victory.

In the second half of the Rose Bowl, Roy was probably the best player on the field. On defense he was everywhere, fighting off blocks and tackling Georgia Tech players all over the field. On offense he snapped the ball like an expert and held his blocks until the ball carrier was tackled. On one occasion Roy led his team in a heroic goal-line stand as they stopped the Yellow Jackets on the one-yard line. On another, as the Yellow Jackets tried to punt, Roy pushed past his counterpart, All-American Peter Pund, and jumped in the air, blocking the ball and giving his team great field possession.

Yet no matter how hard he played, the Golden Bears just couldn't score. At one point Benny Lom picked up a fumble and ran for an apparent touchdown, but there was a penalty on the play and Georgia Tech got to keep the ball.

The Yellow Jackets finally broke through for a touchdown in the third quarter. First back Warner Mizell swept the end for forty yards. Then on the next play Stumpy Thomason burst into the end zone. Georgia missed the extra point, but now led 8–0.

The Golden Bears didn't quit, however. Late in the fourth quarter Benny Lom completed several long passes and the Bears drove far down the field. With one minute remaining they scored a touchdown when Lom lofted a pass to Irving Phillips. The extra point made the score 8–7.

California decided to try an onside kick on the kickoff, booting the ball only a few yards, then hoping to recover it themselves and have another chance to score, but Georgia Tech recovered the football. They were able to run out the clock and won the ballgame 8–7. The difference in the game had been the safety after Roy Riegels's wrong-way run.

After the game, however, Riegels didn't hide. He held his head high and answered every question newspaper reporters asked of him. He didn't make any excuses, not even when some reporters asked if he had been groggy from being hit in the head a few plays earlier, something Riegels later admitted to his parents might have been true. Instead he simply said, "I completely lost my bearings," and took full responsibility for the play.

The next day Roy Riegels's name was in newspaper headlines all over the country, many of them referring to him by his new nickname. For the rest of his life he would be known as Roy "Wrong Way" Riegels.

No one would have blamed Roy had he decided to quit football and stay out of the limelight, but when Roy went back onto the field after halftime, he made a choice, and he followed through on it. He remained on the team in his senior season, serving as captain, earning all-conference honors, and even being named to several All-American teams. He might have made one mistake, but he proved to everyone he was one of the best football players in the country.

After graduating from the University of California, Roy coached football for a few years, first for the freshman team at the University of California, then at a junior high and high school. He married, had four children, and served in the Army Air Force as a major in World War II; he then went to work for a cannery and eventually started his own successful company. He didn't try to hide from who he was, and over time learned to laugh at what happened, once telling a reporter, "Sometimes my ten-year-old son calls me 'Wrong Way' Riegels."

"I used to be sensitive," he explained, "but everybody else thought it was funny and I finally decided all I could do was laugh with them." One time when Roy appeared on a television program, he even agreed to start to walk off the stage the wrong way, making everyone laugh. And when Georgia Tech decided to induct the entire 1928 Yellow Jackets team into their Hall of Fame, Roy accepted an invitation to attend the ceremony.

Roy Riegels knew he couldn't escape what happened that day, but, even more impressively, he did not try to. In fact, Roy continued to demonstrate that failure isn't nearly as important as how one reacts to it.

Every few years, some unfortunate high school football player would make the same mistake Roy did, and after a fumble or an interception take off running in the wrong direction. As soon as Roy heard about it, he would send the young man a letter or telegram. Here is what he wrote to one young high school player who intercepted a pass and ran it back fifty-five yards into his own end zone:

Dear Jan,

Don't let one bad run spoil your life or even your enjoyment of the football season.

So you made a mistake. They make a lot of them in football. After all, you were playing to win. And you must be a pretty good player or you wouldn't be in there doing the job. . . . For many years I've had to go along and laugh whenever my wrong way run was brought up . . . it certainly wasn't the most serious thing in the world. I regretted doing it, even as you do, but you'll get over it. . . . Let's get back together in four–five years . . . and we'll have a good laugh together.

Your friend,

Roy Riegels

Roy Riegels may once have run the wrong way on a football field, but off the field, where it was more important, he did almost everything else right. They might have called him "Wrong Way" Riegels after that game, but no one ever called him a loser.

The Buffalo Bills quarterback Frank Reich and kicker Steve Christie celebrate after Christie's field goal caps the Bills' stunning comeback.

ONE LAST CHANCE

SOMETIMES, ALL YOU NEED IS a chance.

As he was growing up in Lebanon, Pennsylvania, Frank Reich, like most other young boys, dreamed of being a sports star. During baseball season he imagined getting the big hit to win the World Series. When basketball season began he pictured himself making the last-second shot.

Most of the time, however, Frank dreamed of playing football. His father, also Frank, had been a star linebacker and center in nearby Steelton, Pennsylvania, where he led his high school team to two Central Pennsylvania League titles. Frank's father then attended Penn State University, where he won three varsity letters and was named to Penn

State's all-decade team for the 1950s. He later became the head football coach at Lebanon High School.

Like his father, Frank was a talented athlete. Tall and strong, in his junior and senior seasons he was starting quarterback for Cedar Crest High School in Lebanon and played well enough to earn honorable mention as quarterback on the All-State team. He was also selected to play in the "Big 33" football classic, a high school all-star game known as the Super Bowl of high school games. After high school he accepted a football scholarship to the University of Maryland and set his sights on playing professional football and becoming an NFL star.

During his first year at Maryland, Frank was asked to "red shirt," meaning that although he would be allowed to practice with the team, he would not be eligible to play in the games. Maryland had too many quarterbacks already, including senior starter Mike Tice. Maryland coach Bobby Ross knew Frank wouldn't have much of a chance to play and wanted him to gain experience. Frank agreed. After sitting out a year he would still have his four full years of eligibility in college.

In his second year Reich looked forward to competing for the starting job, but he was not the only talented quarterback on the team roster. Boomer Esiason, who after sitting out a year as a red shirt himself had spent one season backing up Mike Tice, was also hoping to become the starting quarterback. Although Frank was talented, in almost every way Esiason was just a little better. He had a stronger arm, was a better runner, and had more experience. In practice before the start of the season, Esiason won the starting job. For the next three years he was one of the best quarterbacks in the history of Maryland football and one of the best college quarterbacks in the nation.

As he sat on the bench behind Esiason week after week without getting a chance to play, Frank's dream of playing in the NFL seemed out of reach. Although he and Boomer were best friends, Frank still wanted to play.

After the 1983 season Esiason was drafted by the Cincinnati Bengals in the NFL, and in his senior year Frank beat out teammate Stan Gelbaugh for the starting spot as Maryland's quarterback. At last, in his final college season, he would get a chance to play. He was determined to make the most of this opportunity. He knew that if he played well he still might get the attention of an NFL team.

Unfortunately, only four games into the season, Frank separated his shoulder, and Stan Gelbaugh took over as starting quarterback. The Maryland Terrapins played well while Frank was out and even after his shoulder healed,

Gelbaugh, a junior, remained the starting quarterback. Frank was afraid he might never get another chance to play.

Late in the year, however, the Terrapins traveled to Miami, Florida, to play the powerful University of Miami Hurricanes. Led by All-American quarterback Bernie Kosar, the Hurricanes were one of the most potent teams in college football. In the first half Kosar carved up the Maryland defense, passing for over two hundred yards, throwing three touchdown passes, and leading his team to a commanding 31–0 lead. At halftime, Maryland coach Bobby Ross decided to pull Stan Gelbaugh from the game and give Frank another chance at quarterback.

Frank Reich knew he had nothing to lose and was determined to play his best. On his third play from scrimmage he threw a thirty-nine-yard touchdown pass to put Maryland on the board and make the score 31–7.

Incredibly, for the rest of the game Frank played the best football of his brief collegiate career. He stayed calm and patient, hitting passes when it mattered most, including two more touchdown tosses, and led Maryland to an incredible 42–40 victory in one of the greatest comebacks in the history of college football.

He learned a valuable lesson that day. As he said later,

he learned that to lead a team from behind, "You don't have to play bombs away" and throw the ball on every down. He simply stayed in his team's offense and took advantage of what the defense gave him, using runs and shorter passes to move the ball instead of trying to throw for a touchdown on every play. NFL scouts took notice of his smart play and after the season, Frank was selected in the third round of the draft by the Buffalo Bills, the fifty-seventh player picked overall. Frank would have the chance to fulfill his dream.

The Bills, however, had other plans for Reich. They already had a quarterback, Jim Kelly, and had decided that Kelly—only one year older than Reich—would become a star. For most of the next seven years, Frank played the same role for the Bills behind Kelly that he had played for Maryland behind Boomer Esiason, who had gone on to become a star with the Cincinnati Bengals.

Frank was a backup quarterback, pure and simple. During practice each week he spent most of his time running plays with the second-team offense. He sat in on strategy meetings and took a few snaps with the first team just in case he had to play. Then each Sunday he stood on the sidelines and helped signal the plays to Jim Kelly. His job was to stay ready in case Kelly was injured or some other emergency kept him out of the lineup. Reich knew that if something terrible happened and Kelly's career came to an end, he was unlikely to be the starting quarterback for long. The Bills liked Frank, but had decided he was a backup quarterback and would probably look for another starter.

Kelly was rugged and rarely got hurt. In his first two seasons, Frank got a chance to play in only four games and threw only twenty passes. After the 1987 season, he was released and didn't play at all in 1988, but he returned to the Bills in 1989. Over the next few seasons he played well in the few opportunities that came his way as the Bills became a perennial contender for the NFL championship, winning their division title in 1990 and 1991.

Frank had earned a reputation as a dependable backup quarterback. Although he wasn't very flashy, he knew Buffalo's offense. When he got to play he made few mistakes and usually gave his team a chance to win. Though many Buffalo fans didn't even know his name, Frank was a valuable member of the Bills and someone his teammates believed in.

In 1992 the Bills limped through the end of the season, dropping three of their last five games. In the last game of the regular season, against the Houston Oilers, Jim Kelly injured his knee. Frank took over but didn't play very well, and the Bills lost 27–3. Although the defeat caused the Bills to lose the division title to the Miami Dolphins in a tie-breaker, they made the playoffs as a wild card team. Before Kelly had been injured, Bills fans and football observers had believed Buffalo had a chance to reach the Super Bowl. Now, with Kelly out, few people thought that was likely.

The playoffs began on January 3, 1993. On that cold, gray, blustery day, the Bills once again had to play the Houston Oilers.

For the Bills, the first half was a blur. Despite a stiff wind blowing down the field, Houston quarterback Warren Moon shredded the Buffalo defense, completing nineteen of twenty-two passes and throwing for four touchdowns. Meanwhile, Frank and the Buffalo offense had hardly moved the ball.

When the referee blew his whistle marking the end of the first half, the boos from the crowd at Buffalo's Rich Stadium told the story. The Oilers already led 28–3. Fans were convinced it was over. As the Bills trudged off the field to the locker room, some fans turned for the exits.

No one blamed them for leaving on such a cold day when their team was so far behind. With a backup quarterback running the team, a comeback seemed impossible. Not only was Jim Kelly out, but star linebacker Cornelius Bennett had pulled a muscle in his leg and All-Pro running back Thurman Thomas had hurt his hip. Besides, not only did the Oilers have the best passing offense in the league, but their defense was the third best in the NFL. Nine players on the team had been named to the Pro Bowl squads. Nothing was going right for the Bills. Anyone who believed that Frank Reich would lead the Bills to a comeback against the powerful Oilers was dreaming.

As the Bills sat in the locker room during halftime, Coach Marv Levy tried to fire up his team, telling them, "You've got thirty more minutes. Maybe it's the last thirty minutes of your season. When your season's over, you're going to have to live with yourselves and look yourselves in the eyes. You'd better have reason to feel good about yourselves, regardless of how this game turns out." The players listened, but few believed they had a chance to win.

But Frank Reich knew the situation wasn't hopeless. He remembered the big comeback he had led against the University of Miami. In fact, the Bills' third-string quarterback, Gale Gilbert, even went up to Frank at halftime and told him, "Hey, you did this in college. You can do this here."

Frank was thinking the same thing. He might have been the only person in the stadium who still believed a comeback was possible. He knew that if he remained patient and didn't play "bombs away," the Bills could still come back. There was no reason to give up yet.

The Bills took the kickoff to start the second half and started marching down the field. Then a bad situation got worse. Reich fired a pass to tight end Keith McKeller down the right sideline, but as McKeller reached for the ball, it bounced off his hands. Oilers safety Bubba McDowell plucked the ball from the air, tucked it under his arm, and started running down the sideline. Fifty-eight yards and a few seconds later he reached the end zone. The extra point made the score 35–3.

On the Oilers' sideline players were giving each other high-fives and laughing. A radio announcer told listeners, "The lights are on here at Rich Stadium, they've been on since this morning, and you could pretty much turn them out on the Bills right now." They way things were going, the Bills were in danger of becoming the laughingstock of the league.

Frank Reich was discouraged, but he still wasn't ready to quit. He knew he had made a good pass — his tight end had just missed it. Teammate after teammate came up to him on the sidelines and offered encouragement. As they did, Reich told them, "We just have to take this one play at a time. That's the only thing we can do." That was true, and it was the right thing to say, but no team in NFL history had ever come back to win after being behind by thirty-two points in the second half.

The Oilers were sure they had the game won. As Houston quarterback Warren Moon said later, "We had control of this game like no one has ever had control of a game." But when Houston kicker Al Del Greco kicked off after the touchdown, the wind blew the ball from the tee just as his foot struck the ball. Instead of soaring downfield, the ball bounced crazily for only a few yards. A Buffalo player jumped on the ball at midfield and the Bills took over at the fifty-yard line.

Frank knew there was no way he could score thirty-three points on one long pass. He just tried to move the Bills down the field. At the same time, the Oilers changed their defensive approach. They expected the Bills to try to score quickly on long passes. So instead of playing aggressively, they backed off a little bit and were willing to give up short gains in order to stop the long pass. Their defensive backs played a little deeper, their linebackers stopped blitzing, and their defensive linemen stopped rushing as hard as they had in the first half. The game wasn't over, but the Oilers were already looking ahead to their next playoff game, trying to save energy and not get hurt.

Frank recognized that the Oilers had backed off and remained patient. He put together a ten-play drive of runs and short passes that ended with running back Ken Davis dashing around the left end for a touchdown. Now the score was 35–10.

The Bills still had nothing to lose. Coach Levy decided to take a chance on the kickoff. Instead of asking Steve Christie to kick the ball deep downfield, he ordered him to try an onside kick.

After a kick travels ten yards, it is a free ball and can be picked up by either team. An onside kick is when the kicking team purposely kicks the ball only a short distance, hoping to recover it. Onside kicks are rarely successful, and when they fail they give the other team great field position.

The Oilers should have been prepared for such a kick and sent in their onside kicking team, one made up of players like running backs and wide receivers who are accustomed to handling the ball. Instead, the Oilers thought the Bills had given up, and they sent out their usual team composed primarily of players unaccustomed to catching the ball.

When the referee signaled him to kick off, Steve Christie jogged slowly toward the ball as if he were going to kick it far downfield, then pulled up and kicked the top of the ball, barely grazing it. The ball bounced and hopped forward crazily, then caromed off a Houston player ten yards down the field. The Bills and Oilers scrambled for possession, but Christie saw the ball squirt free and slid into the pile, wrapping his arms around the ball and holding on tight.

The referees peeled players off the pile and then one dramatically pointed his arm toward the Buffalo end zone. The play had worked! Buffalo had the ball again.

On the Bills' sideline, the players looked at one another. As injured quarterback Jim Kelly later recalled, "Everybody's eyes opened up real wide." The Bills were starting to believe they had a chance. And on the Oilers' sideline, there was suddenly confusion. Players began to argue with each other about whether the right kicking team had been on the field. They weren't laughing anymore.

Frank Reich tried to take advantage of the Oilers defense. On the fourth play after Buffalo took over, wide receiver Frank Beebe streaked down the left sideline. As he did, Houston defensive back Jerry Gray bumped him out of bounds. Once a player goes out of bounds, he is not allowed to come back in and catch a pass.

Beebe, however, didn't realize he had stepped out of bounds. Neither did Frank Reich or the referee, who was looking the other way. And after bumping Beebe, Jerry Gray had slowed down. Frank saw that Beebe was running free behind the defense and lofted a long pass toward the receiver, who continued running his pass route. By the time the ball came down, Beebe was wide open. He gathered in the thirty-eight-yard pass and loped into the end zone for a touchdown. The extra point made the score 35–17.

As Bills center Ken Hill said later, "The momentum shifted our way at that point. You could feel it." After all, the third quarter was only half over, and now the Bills trailed by only eighteen points. There was still plenty of time left in the game.

This time the Bills kicked off deep to Houston, and the Oilers got the ball for the first time in the second half. Suddenly, however, the Buffalo defense that until now had been so easy to move the ball on stiffened, and the Oilers, who had passed the ball so successfully in the first half, tried to run instead. The fired-up defense held and forced the Oilers to punt for the first time all game. The Bills took over at their forty-one-yard line.

Now the Oilers were beginning to panic. Instead of playing confidently, they became tentative. Reich had found his rhythm and calmly threw an eighteen-yard pass to receiver James Lofton. Then running back Ken Davis rumbled another nineteen yards on a screen play to put the Bills on the Houston twenty-six-yard line.

Buffalo wide receiver Andre Reed, after averaging nine touchdowns a year for the previous three seasons, had scored only three times during the 1992 regular season. Before the game he had told Reich, "You've got to get me the ball today. It's time. It's the playoffs. The chips are down."

Now Frank remembered Reed's words. As the ball was snapped the receiver raced downfield, first faking to the inside before breaking to the sideline. The defender followed his fake to the inside, and when Reed turned around at the five-yard line he was all alone. Reich rifled a pass into his chest. Reed was so wide open that he stumbled into the end zone backwards. After the extra point the score was suddenly 35–24. Buffalo had scored three touchdowns in only four and a half minutes of play!

As one Houston player said later, "It seemed like time was standing still, like they were scoring every fifteen or twenty seconds." Now the Bills weren't just hoping to make the game close, they were hoping to win. They stood on the sidelines and waved their arms and towels over their heads to get the crowd going. The few thousand fans still inside Rich Stadium suddenly sounded like sixty thousand. Fans in their cars listening to the game on the radio turned around and went back to the stadium.

The Oilers took the kickoff and decided to pass the ball again. But now Warren Moon was as cold as he had been hot in the first half. His pass to Webster Slaughter went off the receiver's fingertips. Bills defensive back Henry Jones grabbed the errant ball and raced downfield, returning the ball nearly twenty yards to the Houston twenty-four-yard line.

Now the Bills turned conservative, gaining only five yards on three plays.

Coach Levy later recalled that a few minutes earlier he had told the other coaches, "If we hit a fourth down we're going for it . . . the reasoning was that if we made the field goal we were still down by eight. The quarter was nearly over and we'd be going against the wind in the fourth quarter and we would have to get very close to try a field goal." Besides, he had Frank Reich at quarterback, and thus far in the second half, Frank had been on fire.

Since Andre Reed had scored by faking inside and going outside, this time the Bills called a play for Reed on the inside. When he broke toward the middle, the defender, thinking it was a fake, let him go. Reich dropped back and saw Reed open in the middle of the field.

With defenders closing from all directions, Reich's pass found Reed's hands as Reed dove for the ball just over the end zone. The referee's arms shot into the air as Reed slid along the ground, hugging the football. Touchdown!

Less than seven minutes earlier the Bills had trailed by thirty-one points. Now they trailed by only three, 35–32.

As if exhausted by the pace of play, on their next possessions neither team could move the ball. Then, in the fourth quarter, the Oilers got the ball back. With the wind at his back, Warren Moon was suddenly effective again and drove his team deep downfield, eating up more than seven minutes on the drive. The Oilers knew that if they could score, there wouldn't be much time left for the Bills to catch up.

The Bills defense held firm, however, and on fourth down with the ball on the fourteen-yard line, the Oilers decided to try a thirty-one-yard field goal.

As the Oilers lined up for the kick it started to rain. The

holder, Greg Montgomery, tried to get the referee's attention to ask him to wipe off the ball, but the ref whistled for the play to start. The center snapped the ball just as a big gust of wind blew across the field.

Instead of the snap going straight into Montgomery's hands, the wind lifted it a bit high, and the wet ball squirted through his fingers.

There was a mad scramble for the ball, and a Buffalo player picked it up and raced downfield. For a moment it looked as if he would score, but the referee ruled that the ball was dead. Still, it was Buffalo's ball and just over seven minutes remained in the game.

After two plays the Bills were still four yards short of a first down. Coach Levy sent in a pass play, but Frank Reich didn't like it and called a time-out.

He trotted over to the sidelines and met with his coach. "I wanted to know whether we were going to go for it on fourth down," he said later. "Marv said we probably would, so I said, 'Why not try to run for it. They won't be expecting it.'"

Levy agreed. Frank called another draw play, a run designed to look like a pass to Ken Davis. The ball was snapped, Reich dropped back as if to pass, then handed the ball to Davis as the defense dropped back into pass coverage. Davis broke through a huge hole on the right side and rumbled up the field for thirty-five yards, putting the ball at the Houston thirty-three.

A few plays later the Bills called for another pass to Reed. It was like Frank and Reed were reading each other's minds. The receiver expertly worked his way free and Reich threw a perfect pass, just out of the reach of several defenders, and Reed caught the ball in full stride to the end zone. He spiked the ball in celebration as the Bills crowd erupted in cheers.

Incredibly, the Bills were now ahead, 38–35, and Frank Reich, the backup quarterback, had led them all the way!

But the game wasn't quite over. There were still three minutes left to play, and if the Oilers scored a touchdown, they could win the game.

Warren Moon wasn't about to give up. He worked his team down the field and completed a key pass on fourth down that put the ball within field goal range. With only twelve seconds remaining, kicker Al Del Greco came out to try a twenty-six-yard field goal to tie the game. This time the snap was good, and Del Greco's kick sailed through the uprights. A few moments later the clock ran out, sending the game into sudden death overtime.

The Oilers won the coin toss and elected to receive the ball. The Bills took the wind, forcing the Oilers to throw against the stiff breeze.

On the third play from scrimmage, Moon threw downfield. His receiver was tripped up, the ball floated high, and the Bills' Nate Odomes intercepted the ball. As he was tackled an Oiler player grabbed his face mask, earning a fifteen-yard penalty that easily put the Bills within field goal range.

Now the Bills played cautiously, running the ball twice. Then Coach Levy sent in Steve Christie to attempt a field goal. If he made the kick, the Bills would win.

Frank Reich crouched on the ground behind the center, barking out the signals. The ball was snapped. Frank snatched it from the air and swiftly placed the point on the ground, holding the ball upright for his kicker. Christie took a few quick steps and hit the ball square.

It tumbled end over end right between the uprights. The referees threw their hands in the air.

The kick was good! The Bills won, 41–38! All over the field, the Bills jumped into each other's arms in celebration, scarcely believing the final score. The Oilers, meanwhile, looked to the ground in disappointment. Frank Reich and the Bills had done the impossible!

Nearly two decades later, that game is still considered the greatest comeback in the history of the NFL. The following week, Frank Reich led the Bills to another playoff win over Pittsburgh; then Jim Kelly returned to the lineup and Buffalo defeated the Miami Dolphins to earn the right to play in the Super Bowl against the Dallas Cowboys.

Jim Kelly started the game, but with the Bills trailing 14–7, he reinjured his knee. Frank again stepped in. But although he played well, this time there was no comeback, and the Bills lost, 52–17.

Frank Reich went on to play another six years in the NFL for the Bills, Carolina Panthers, New York Jets, and Detroit Lions, primarily as a backup quarterback. Although he never led another team to a comeback as spectacular as that against the Houston Oilers, each time a team that falls far behind is given "no chance" of winning, someone usually brings up the story of Frank Reich and the Buffalo Bills, a player and a team who made the most of their chances.

The Houston Rockets forward Tracy McGrady (1) shoots over the San Antonio Spurs' Bruce Bowen (12).

THE LONG SHOT

NBA STAR FORWARD TRACY MCGRADY, known to basketball
fans as "T-Mac," had it all. Well, almost all.

At the end of the 2003–2004 season, McGrady was at
the top of his game. Already a three-time All-Star, McGrady
had led the league in scoring for two consecutive seasons,
most recently with an average of more than twenty-eight
points a game, including a career high of an astounding
sixty-two points in one game. *SLAM* magazine had already
ranked McGrady as one of the "top seventy-five players of
all time." As adept at dunking the ball as he was at shooting from behind the three-point arc, at six foot eight and
quick as a cat, T-Mac could do just about anything on a
basketball court well.

Off the court he was just as successful, earning millions of dollars a season, living in an enormous house, taking care of his children and family, and giving money to a variety of charities. At the age of twenty-five, McGrady was at the peak of his career.

Yet there was one thing Tracy McGrady did not have—the respect of his peers and the NBA fans. While everyone acknowledged his talent, for all his skills, some questioned whether he made his team better. As one NBA general manager said, "A superstar is defined by wins, by making players around him better and by making the team better." Tracy McGrady had not quite done that. In seven NBA seasons his teams had often been a disappointment, not winning as often as they should and not advancing very far in the playoffs. Although the perception didn't tell the whole story—basketball is a team game and the impact of one player, even a superstar, is limited—even McGrady admitted that he had something to prove. "I'm not going to say I played my hardest every night," he said later of his performance one season. "Some nights I did slack off, and I knew that was a terrible thing to do." He knew there was only one way to earn the respect he craved—by proving it on the court.

One reason Tracy had yet to do that may have been his up-bringing. Growing up in Auburndale, Florida, Tracy had to learn to do many things by himself. His mother, Melanise, raised Tracy without much help from his father. A maid at Disney World, she and Tracy lived with her mother, Tracy's grandmother.

Tall and wiry, Tracy was just a young boy when he fell in love with sports, particularly baseball. In Little League he was a great hitter and a terrific pitcher. He dreamed of pitching in the major leagues.

In fact, Tracy was so focused on baseball that he didn't even take basketball very seriously, another reason why it might have taken him a bit longer than some other players to learn to play the game and be a good team player. Oh, he liked to play basketball with his friends, but he didn't study the game the same way he did baseball. On the base-ball diamond he could analyze a situation and figure out what to throw a hitter to get him out, but on the basketball court, Tracy just played.

Then in 1993, guard Penny Hardaway joined the NBA's Orlando Magic. Tracy loved the way Hardaway played basketball and wanted to do the same things he did — shoot the lights out of the basket, hit his teammates with precise passes, and handle the ball like a magician. Tracy began to take basketball more seriously, playing in school and for an Amateur Athletic Union (AAU) team in the off-season, and dreaming of a chance to play professionally in the NBA. That was a long shot, but Tracy didn't know that. He just knew what he wanted to do.

Tracy made the basketball team at Auburndale High School, but during his first two seasons, Coach Ty Willis barely let Tracy play for the Bloodhounds. Although Tracy was skilled, other players had more experience and understood the game better. But in his junior year, Tracy, who had grown to nearly his full height, began to stand out, averaging twenty-three points and twelve rebounds a game. Big-time colleges began to take an interest in him and it seemed likely that he would earn a scholarship to play basketball.

Unfortunately, Tracy was not a good student. He often skipped class and didn't take his studies very seriously. Even when he did attend class, he rarely opened a book. Then one day he got into an argument with a teacher and was disrespectful. He was kicked off the basketball team due to the outburst. Most college recruiters considered

Tracy a troublemaker and forgot all about him. His dream to play in the NBA dimmed.

Fortunately, his AAU coach was able to get Tracy invited to the ABCD summer basketball camp, one of the best basketball camps in the country. Nearly every player at the camp was far better known than Tracy, who was not even considered one of the five hundred best high school players in America.

At the camp, in addition to taking instruction, players were divided into teams and played against one another in scrimmages. Many college coaches attend such camps so they can see talented high school players compete against other kids just as talented. Tracy's reputation — and his future — depended on how well he played.

Since getting kicked off the basketball team, Tracy had been working hard. Not only had his game improved, but he had grown faster and stronger. In one scrimmage at the camp, Tracy asked to be matched up opposite Lamar Odom. At the time Odom was already well known to most basketball fans. Big and fast and with enough skill to play any position on the court, he was considered the best high school player in the country. Most players at the camp didn't want anything to do with either guarding Odom or trying to score against him. Compared to Odom, Tracy was a nobody, so he knew he had nothing to lose by playing against Odom. Tracy needed to stand out, and this was his chance.

Odom made Tracy a somebody. T-Mac dominated Odom on both offense and defense, made the camp all-star team, and in the camp all-star game threw down a monster windmill dunk over another well-known prospect. "After I made that dunk," said Tracy later, "I had chills running through my body." After the camp, Tracy, the prospect no one knew about, was suddenly considered one of the best high school–age basketball players in the country. Once he really learned the game, there was no telling how good he might become.

But Tracy still had a lot of growing to do as a person. His grades weren't good enough for college and he still had to prove that he was not a troublemaker. Based on his performance at camp, Tracy received a scholarship offer from a private high school, Mount Zion Christian Academy in North Carolina. He would have one year to get serious, both as a basketball player and as a person.

Under Coach Joe Hopkins and the disciplined structure of Mount Zion, Tracy thrived. Coach Hopkins was strict, but for the first time in his life Tracy had someone to teach him not just how to play the game, but how to act and behave. Although the player and coach clashed at first and on one occasion almost had a fistfight, Tracy finally began to grow up. The Mighty Warriors of Mount Zion finished the season with a 20–1 record and were ranked the second-best high school team in the country. Tracy, who averaged more than twenty-seven points a game, was named the *USA Today* high school Player of the Year and was selected for the prestigious McDonald's High School All-American team. Even his grades improved, and Tracy later credited Coach Hopkins with turning his life around, saying, "He's my backbone." At the end of the season Tracy was offered a scholarship to the University of Kentucky, home to one of the best college basketball programs in the country.

Then the NBA came calling. Through his coach and advisors, Tracy learned that if he entered the NBA draft he would likely be a top pick and receive a contract worth millions of dollars. On the other hand, if he went to college, there was always the risk that he could get hurt and never have another chance to play pro basketball. It was a tough decision, but Tracy decided to enter the draft. The Toronto Raptors selected him with the ninth pick of the first round. The long shot had come through.

This was both the best thing and the worst thing that could have happened. On the one hand, Tracy was suddenly wealthy, able to take care of his family and help out others. On the other hand, he was entering the NBA with a lot of talent but not much experience. Moreover, when Tracy first joined them, the Toronto Raptors were a terrible team.

Tracy's three seasons with the Raptors proved to be a mixed blessing. At first he hardly played. He learned that he had to earn game time by playing well in practice. He also had to work out more, to get stronger and work on all his skills. It helped when in his second season he learned that Raptors star rookie Vince Carter was, in fact, his second cousin. The two became fast friends and Carter, who had gone to college before entering the NBA, helped Tracy adjust. By the end of his third year Tracy was beginning to see significant playing time and averaged more than fifteen points per game. The Raptors were improving and even made the playoffs.

Yet at the same time, Tracy didn't learn as much about team play as he might have with another team or in college. He was skilled, but still had more to learn.

At the end of his third season Tracy's contract was up and he was scheduled to become a free agent, meaning any team in the league could sign him to a new contract. Despite his shortcomings, Tracy was still one of the most talented players in the league and everyone knew he had yet to fulfill his potential.

Tracy hoped to go back to Florida, and the Raptors and the Orlando Magic, Tracy's favorite team growing up, worked out a deal. Tracy re-signed with Toronto for seven years with the understanding he would be traded to the Magic as soon as he signed. The Magic also signed All-Star Grant Hill, and Tracy thought he and Hill could lead the Magic to a championship.

Unfortunately, early in his first season with the Magic, Hill was injured, and Tracy became a one-man show for the team. He averaged over twenty points a game, was named the league's Most Improved Player, and took the team to the playoffs, but he couldn't do everything. The Magic lost in the first round.

The next few years followed the same pattern. Hill never really came back from his injury and Tracy remained the focus of the Magic's offense. He became a scoring wizard, often leading the team in assists and rebounds, and became known as a complete player, but nothing he did was enough. Just as the great Michael Jordan was unable to lead the Chicago Bulls to a championship by himself, neither could Tracy McGrady do this for Orlando. For several years in a row the Magic kept making the playoffs — barely — and then were bounced out in the first round as the other team simply focused on trying to shut down Tracy. They rarely succeeded, but Tracy's teammates were unable to pick up the slack.

In 2004 injuries hit the Magic and after an opening night victory, the team collapsed, losing nineteen games in a row. Even as Tracy lit up the scoreboard, winning another scoring title, some fans and NBA observers complained that Tracy wasn't doing everything he could to help the team win games. Given all the injuries on the team, there was little he could do, but the criticism still stung. Tracy also knew that at times he was so frustrated he didn't try to do his best.

At the end of the season the Magic decided to rebuild, and they made Tracy available to other teams by way of a trade. That was fine with Tracy — he just wanted a chance to win and prove his critics wrong. The Magic entertained offers from several clubs before finally dealing Tracy to the Houston Rockets.

McGrady was thrilled. The Rockets featured several talented players, including forward Juwan Howard and towering center Yao Ming. Maybe, thought Tracy, he was finally with a team that had the ability to win.

Only a few weeks into the 2004–2005 season, however, that hope seemed like a distant dream. As the seconds ticked off the clock near the end of the fourth quarter of a game on December 9, 2004, between the Rockets and their archrivals, the cross-state San Antonio Spurs, one Rockets fan after another got up and headed for the parking lot.

The Spurs, defending Western Conference champions and winners of the NBA championship only two seasons before, had beaten the Rockets in their last seven meetings. In a few moments, that streak seemed likely to increase to eight. The Rockets were playing terrible basketball, and with just over a minute left to play they trailed the Spurs by ten points, 74–64. It felt like they trailed by thirty. The Rockets were not only about to lose, but were on pace to finish with one of the lowest point totals in franchise history.

Many fans blamed the team's performance on Tracy Mc-Grady. Rockets fans had high expectations and expected instant results, but so far the Rockets — and McGrady — had struggled. The team just didn't seem able to play together. Although Tracy had put up some remarkable numbers — in one contest against the Dallas Mavericks, he had scored forty-eight points — the Rockets just couldn't seem to win.

In fact, despite McGrady's forty-eight points that day they had lost to the Mavericks, as Dirk Nowitzki had scored fifty-three points for Dallas.

The performance against the Spurs was yet another disappointment. After starting strong and taking an 18–12 lead at the end of the first quarter, the Rockets had slowly fallen behind. The Spurs' Bruce Bowen, one of the best defensive players in the NBA, had shut Tracy down. McGrady was ice cold, making only eight of twenty-four shots, including only one of eight three-pointers. Had he managed to make even made half of his shots, the Rockets might have been ahead. Instead, they seemed likely to lose yet again and drop their record to a dismal 8–12 for the season.

With only fifty-five seconds on the clock, Tracy dribbled the ball at the top of the key. Once again Bowen played Tracy close, not wanting him to take a three-point shot that could get the Rockets back into the game.

Unable to get off a three-pointer, Tracy drove to the basket and tossed up a wild, running hook. Rockets fans groaned.

The ball glanced high off the backboard for a miss, but fortunately Yao Ming was in perfect position for the rebound. He grabbed the ball and thundered it through the hoop for a dunk. When the Spurs passed the ball in, another Rockets player stole the pass and threw down another dunk to make the score 74–68. With less than fifty seconds remaining, the Rockets still seemed likely to lose, but at least the score would look more respectable.

The Spurs inbounded the ball again and moved the ball down the court. Devin Brown got the ball in the corner and Tracy tried for a steal, his arm swiping at the ball. The referee called a foul on McGrady and some Houston fans threw up their arms in disgust. Brown sank both shots and the Spurs' lead was back to eight points.

The game was all but over, but Tracy, disappointed in his play, was determined to finish strong. To give the Rockets a chance, he knew he would have to hit some long shots.

Tracy took the ball in the backcourt and dribbled up the left side, trying to find an opening as Bowen guarded him close. After he crossed half court Tracy tried to drive to the basket but was cut off. He spun and dribbled across the top of the key as the Spurs switched defenders.

That was a mistake. Suddenly Tracy was open. He leapt into the air and fired a long jump shot. The ball swished through the rim for a three-pointer, making the score 76–71. There were now thirty-five seconds left in the game.

Desperate to get the ball back, Rockets point guard Bob Sura quickly fouled one of the Spurs, hoping he would miss the free throws and the Rockets would get the ball back. But the Spurs player calmly sank both shots, giving San Antonio a 78–71 lead with only thirty-one seconds left. Now the game was *really* over.

The Rockets inbounded the ball and put it in Tracy's hands. With Bowen all over him again, McGrady dribbled across half court, and then bobbled the ball at the top of the key, nearly losing control. But he managed to regain his dribble.

Meanwhile, Yao Ming came out to help. He stood just outside the three-point circle to McGrady's right, setting up what is known as a screen. If Tracy dribbled the ball closely past Yao Ming, Bowen, with Ming in the way, would not be able to follow him.

Tracy saw Ming and did just that, breaking into the open for a moment in his favorite spot, just outside the three-point line and a few steps to the right.

But the Spurs All-Star center Tim Duncan, one of the best shot blockers in the league, saw what was happening. He took a few quick strides and was suddenly in Tracy's face.

Tracy could have gone straight up for a three-point shot, but he knew the Rockets had to score as many points as possible. If he made the shot and was fouled in the process, he would have the opportunity to take a foul shot afterwards and make a rare four-point play.

So instead of shooting right away, Tracy lifted the ball over his head as if to shoot, and then pulled it back down. Duncan jumped, Tracy leaned in, and just as the Spurs center came down and banged into him, Tracy launched an awkward-looking shot from his shoulder. The ball didn't even hit the rim as the three-pointer went in.

Then the referee blew his whistle, signaled that the shot was good, and called a foul on Duncan! The Spurs' star rolled his eyes, scarcely believing he had been fooled by Tracy.

For almost the first time all game, the few Rocket fans who remained in the arena erupted in cheers. Tracy calmly stepped to the line, dribbled once, and sank the foul shot to complete the four-point play. With twenty-four seconds left the score was now 78–75.

The Spurs called a time-out. They wanted to make sure everyone on the team knew what to do next. The Rockets were certain to foul to try to get the ball back, and the Spurs would try their best not to let that happen.

The Spurs inbounded the ball and played "keep away" for eight seconds, passing the ball all over the court before the Rockets managed to foul.

But when the Spurs sank the next two foul shots to make the score 80–75 with only sixteen seconds left, the game truly seemed over. There seemed no way the Rockets could catch up. They were simply running out of time.

Still, Houston called time so they could inbound the ball in the frontcourt. Andre Barrett desperately looked for an open player before tossing the ball back toward Tracy just inside the half-court line.

The pass was high and two defenders were draped over him, but Tracy managed to reach up and over both men, came down with the ball, and started dribbling again to his favorite spot. Bruce Bowen knew what Tracy was trying to do and followed him like a shadow.

Still, Tracy got to the spot first. Then he launched himself into the air as Bowen, a split second later, tried to block his shot.

For the third time in a row Tracy's three-pointer swished through the hoop without touching the rim. The score was 80–78! Rockets fans sat in stunned disbelief. Some cheered and others looked at each other wide-eyed, unable to believe what they were seeing. Somehow, in the last thirty-eight seconds, the Rockets had scored an amazing fourteen points. In the last twenty seconds Tracy McGrady, by himself, had scored ten points, and now the Rockets trailed by only two. Eleven seconds remained in the game.

San Antonio called time out again. They had to figure out some way to keep Tracy from getting the ball. The entire crowd stood as both teams huddled. They sensed they were witnessing something special.

Now the Spurs' Brent Barry looked to inbound the ball in the frontcourt as the Rockets dashed all over the place, waving their arms, desperate for a steal. Unless they could steal the ball, they would have to foul again and give the Spurs another chance at the free-throw line.

Devin Brown, San Antonio's best free-throw shooter and one of their best ball handlers, dashed in front of Barry. He was the player the Spurs wanted to have the ball. Barry passed him the basketball, and Brown, knowing he was likely to be fouled, spun toward the corner to try to run some time off the clock, then went toward the basket so he could take a shot in the event he was fouled.

But as he stepped down the baseline, he slipped, falling to the ground and losing control of the ball. Like magic it bounced into the hands of—who else?—Tracy McGrady! There were seven seconds left and the Rockets' basket was eighty feet away.

Tracy sprinted down the court, dribbling the ball. After taking only two strides, Bruce Bowen drew alongside him, careful not to foul but smartly blocking his way from his favorite spot on the right side.

Tracy, feeling the pressure and knowing the clock was ticking, dribbled to his left instead, away from Bowen. Then he pulled up two feet behind the three-point line. In front of him, three Spurs stood like a wall, but Tracy was in the air before any of them could jump up to block his shot. Still, as Tracy reached the top of his leap, a defender's hand was in his face, trying to distract him and block his view.

With three seconds left on the clock, the longest shot of all left Tracy's hands.

Every eye in the arena followed the spinning ball through the air. Time seemed to stop as Tracy floated back to the ground, his eyes fixed on the basket.

Swish! Three-pointer! 81–80 Rockets!

Tracy spun around as the shot went through the basket and punched the air with his fist in celebration, his mouth open in disbelief. But he didn't forget that the game wasn't over. The Spurs quickly inbounded the ball to guard Tony Parker. Tracy managed to get in his way as he threw up an awkward shot. The ball clanged off the rim as time ran out.

The game was over. The Rockets had won. In only

thirty-three seconds Tracy McGrady had scored an incredible thirteen points!

Yao Ming ran up to McGrady and wrapped him in his arms. The Spurs stood around like statues, stunned and spent. McGrady's teammates surrounded him in a group hug, and then they all tumbled to the ground, huge smiles on everyone's faces.

No one had ever seen anything like it. No team in NBA history had ever come back from such a large deficit in such a short time, and no player in NBA history had ever scored so many points in thirty-three seconds.

The celebration in the arena was like Times Square on New Year's Eve. Strangers hugged each other and slapped hands, and confetti rained down on the court.

When Tracy got to his feet a television announcer approached him and asked how he felt.

He looked dazed and didn't know what to say. "I was just trying to do anything to get a shot off," he sputtered, as if even he didn't believe what he had done. Then he collected himself and said, "In situations like that, the best player's got to try to step up and make plays. The shots were falling for me at the end. I don't know how I got them off because Bruce Bowen is the best on the defensive end. My will just took over."

Tracy just looked around in wonder, a big smile on his face. "I've never been a part of anything like this," he said, hardy able to talk "You've got to excuse me." Then he raised his arms in the air, soaking in the cheers of the crowd, and walked off the court, his place in the history of the game secure for all time.

Tracy's performance in the final few seconds of the game is still one of the greatest in NBA history. Even better, however, was the impact it had on his team. The comeback gave the Rockets a spark. They turned their season around to finish 51–31 and make the playoffs, the club's best finish in almost a decade.

Everyone realized that Tracy was the reason. His performance against the Spurs seemed to give him confidence, and he raised his game to another level. Although he didn't lead the league in scoring, he finished in the top ten in almost every statistical category tracked by the league. Although the Rockets once again lost in the playoffs, Tracy played well and was recognized as one of the best all-around players in the league.

The long shot had finally gone straight through the hoop.

David Freese connects to hit a walk-off eleventh-inning home run to win game six of the 2011 World Series.

THE GREATEST COMEBACK?

THE ST. LOUIS CARDINALS HAD no chance — none.

In the ninth inning of game six of the 2011 World Series, down three games to two, trailing 7–5 with two outs and two strikes on the batter, the Cardinals were literally one strike away from defeat. Their opponents, the Texas Rangers, were lined on the top step of the dugout, ready to run out on the field in celebration.

Yet twenty-four hours later, after perhaps the greatest comeback in major league history — make that comebacks — the Cardinals were all piled on top of one another in celebration, the world champions of Major League Baseball.

How did *that* happen?

Most great comebacks require several factors. A team that has been playing badly needs to start playing well and a team that has been playing well needs to start playing poorly. And at least one player needs to step up and come through big. Over the final weeks of the 2011 baseball season and in the World Series that followed, the Cardinals had all three factors in abundance. Their victory was not the result of just one comeback, but several, each more unlikely and implausible than the last.

And, oh yeah, the Cardinals also had one more thing, perhaps the most important quality of all—they believed in each other. Strengthened by faith in their team, they never, ever gave up.

In a sense, the comeback that led the St. Louis Cardinals to the World Championship had actually begun nearly a decade before. That was when a young ballplayer named David Freese made a decision that would not only change his life, but eventually help deliver a World Series title to St. Louis.

David grew up just outside St. Louis in the suburb of Wildwood. He loved baseball and played every chance he got. David was good at the game, a smooth infielder and a high-average hitter. David loved the Cardinals and often dreamed of playing for them when he grew up. Like most kids, he would daydream about things like getting the game-winning hit in the World Series.

But there was one big difference for David. He was good enough that as he grew older and entered high school, his dream had a real chance of coming true. David took baseball seriously and played almost year-round for a number of teams. He took hours and hours of batting practice and thousands of ground balls. Many other kids played baseball, but David worked at it. It was almost like a full-time job. David played on a variety of travel teams and the Freeses toured the country, taking him to tournaments. As his mother, Lynn, once explained, "All we did was travel with him . . . that was our vacation."

The results were obvious. By his senior year of high school David was considered the best shortstop in the state of Missouri. In his final season playing for Lafayette High School, David hit twenty-three home runs with a .533 batting average, a school record even better than that of Philadelphia Phillies' star first baseman Ryan Howard, who also graduated from Lafayette. The University of Missouri offered David a scholarship to play baseball.

Despite his spectacular season, however, David wasn't happy. He had been playing baseball so much and for so long that the game had become a chore, and he no longer enjoyed it. At the end of the season he turned down the scholarship and told his coach he was through with baseball. "It's pretty simple and kind of boring," Freese later told a reporter, "but I just didn't want to play anymore." That was not a surprise to Steve Miller, one of David's high school coaches. "A lot of kids will do that," Miller explained later. "They'll get burned out." For years, David had sacrificed things like going to games as a spectator or attending parties because he felt he had to play baseball, and he was tired.

Neither Miller nor David's parents tried to convince him to continue playing. They knew David would have to make his own decisions. Although David's father later said, "I thought he'd retired permanently," David's mother felt otherwise. As soon as she learned he had quit, she told David's father: "He'll be back." She knew he wouldn't be able to stay away from the game he loved for very long.

Instead of going to the University of Missouri to play baseball, David went as a student to study computer science. The following summer he was working for the maintenance department of the local school department when he visited his old high school. Looking around the school and the grounds, he suddenly realized how much he missed playing ball.

"I said, 'What am I doing?'" Freese later recalled. "Stepping away for a year . . . kind of brought me back to the game and helped me realize how much I missed it.

"I called my mom and said, 'Let's go.'" It was time for David's comeback, the first in a series of unlikely events that would lift the Cardinals to victory.

David transferred to St. Louis Community College at Meramec for two seasons. Playing baseball was fun again, and David played well enough to be named to the second team of the National Junior College Athletic Associations All-American team. He then transferred to a four-year school, the University of South Alabama, and continued his stellar play. The Boston Red Sox noticed and offered David a contract after his first year at USA, but Major League Baseball ruled that David had to be made available in the major league draft and was not yet eligible to sign a professional contract. He played even better during his senior season, becoming an All-American third baseman, and was selected in the ninth round of the 2006 MLB draft by the San Diego Padres. He signed with the Padres and after playing two years in the Padres' minor league system, David was traded to the St. Louis Cardinals, his hometown team.

David was thrilled to join the Cardinals organization

and dreamed of playing for his favorite team in front of his family and friends. That dream came true in September of 2009, when the Cardinals called David up to the major leagues. The kid who once quit baseball had come all the way back. But there were even more comebacks in David's future.

In the spring of 2010 David won the starting job at third base for the Cardinals — and then injured his ankle. He eventually had to undergo surgery and missed the second half of the season. But in the spring of 2011 David regained his starting job.

The Cardinals got off to a slow start in 2011. Before the season was even under way, they lost star pitcher Adam Wainwright to an injury, leaving the starting rotation a little thin. Their other ace, Chris Carpenter, then struggled, as did slugging first baseman Albert Pujols. And just when Pujols started to get hot, their other slugger, outfielder Matt Holliday, was hurt. David Freese, after a hot start of his own, broke his hand when he was hit by a pitch and was knocked out of the lineup. Much of the rest of the lineup was filled with younger players still trying to establish themselves as major league ballplayers, or role players of limited ability. Although Cardinal fans hoped their team would challenge for a world championship, as midseason approached, the Cardinals were struggling to play .500 baseball and stay alive in the National League's Central Division race. Reaching the playoffs, much less making it to the World Series, would be a challenge.

An unlikely hero stepped up and helped keep the Cardinals in the running.

As a member of the Houston Astros from 1999 to 2010, outfielder and first baseman Lance Berkman had been one of the best hitters in the major leagues. Slugging as many as forty-five home runs in a season, and usually knocking in more than a hundred runs and hitting over .300, Berkman made the All-Star team five times as an Astro.

But in 2009 and 2010 he struggled with injuries and his performance slipped. Many people in baseball thought Berkman, who turned thirty-four in 2010, was near the end of his career. Late in the year, however, as the New York Yankees fought for the right to play in the postseason, they traded for Berkman, hoping that he might regain form and provide a spark. But Berkman was a disappointment in New York. He was out of shape, his bat looked slow, and he hit only .255 with one home run in 106 at bats for the Yankees. At the end of the season, the Yankees chose not to offer Berkman a contract, making him a free agent and available to any team in baseball.

Based on his recent performance, few teams were interested in signing Lance Berkman in 2011. However, Cardinals manager Tony LaRussa thought otherwise. He remembered how well Berkman had hit when he was a member of the Astros, and he knew Berkman had been bothered by a sore knee in 2010. He believed that if Berkman could get healthy, he could help the Cardinals.

The Cardinals and LaRussa showed their faith in Lance by signing him to a two-year contract. Although it had been several years since Lance had played the outfield, the Cardinals, who already had an All-Star first baseman, Albert Pujols, told Lance they expected him to play the outfield again.

Lance rehabilitated his sore knee in the off-season, which allowed him to work out hard, and he shed some extra weight. The quick bat that had once earned him the respect of every pitcher in baseball returned. Lance became not only one of the best hitters with the Cardinals, but one of the best hitters in the league in 2011. At midseason he was even named to the National League All-Star team again. While many of his teammates struggled, it was Lance who kept the Cardinals in the race for the division title. Although LaRussa wasn't surprised, he still found Berkman's performance "amazing."

In late July, however, the Milwaukee Brewers got hot. They pulled ahead of the Cardinals and over the next month slowly took command as St. Louis fell back.

On August 26, 2011, the Cardinals' season seemed over. St. Louis, with a record of 69–63, was in second place in the National League's Central Division, nine and a half games behind the Brewers, who showed no signs of cooling off. Over their last twenty games the Cardinals had gone 10–10 and lost six and a half games to the Brewers. The Cardinals' other route to the playoff, winning a wild card berth by finishing with the best record in the league without winning a division, was even less promising. Although the Atlanta Braves were 79–54 and trailed the first-place Philadelphia Phillies by six games in the National League's Eastern Division, that record still put them ten and a half games ahead of the Cardinals in the wild card race.

That same day, a website that used statistics to calculate the odds of each major league team to make the playoffs projected that the chances of the Cardinals making the playoffs by winning either the division or a wild card berth were one in a hundred. In St. Louis, even fans who had remained optimistic all year long saw those odds and began to look forward to next year.

Fortunately, the Cardinals players didn't pay much attention to that forecast. They just kept trying to win games. Yet even they didn't realize that their season was about to turn around.

The Cardinals' comeback began slowly. Although the Brewers continued to play well, the Atlanta Braves, a young team with little experience, began running out of steam. Beginning on August 26, the Braves lost seven of their next ten games. At the same time, the Cardinals got hot. By September 18 the Cardinals trailed Atlanta by only three and a half games. The Cardinals kept playing well, the Braves kept stumbling, and on the final day of the season the two teams were tied for the wild card berth. If the Cardinals beat the Astros and the Braves lost to the Phillies, the Cardinals would make the playoffs.

The Cardinals took care of business, opening the game with five straight hits—the last two by Lance Berkman and David Freese—and scoring five times. Chris Carpenter, who over the last month of the season had been pitching his best baseball of the year, shut out the Astros, and the Cards went on to win 8–0. At the end of the game they retreated to their clubhouse to watch the Braves play the Phillies. The game was tied at 3–3 and stayed that way until the thirteenth inning when, with two on and two out, the Phillies' Hunter Pence hit a squibbler to short right field to win the game. The Cardinals broke out in celebration. They were going to the playoffs and would face the Phillies in the first round.

No one gave them a chance against the mighty Phillies, who led the National League with 102 victories and — with Cliff Lee, Cole Hamels, and Roy Halladay — had the best starting pitching in baseball, but the Cardinals didn't care. Despite falling behind Philadelphia two games to one in the series, St. Louis came back again to win the division series in five games as Chris Carpenter outdueled Halladay 1–0 in the final game.

Now the Cardinals had to play the Brewers for the right to face the American League champions in the World Series. Although the Cardinals lost the first game of the series, they stormed back to defeat the Brewers in six games.

The Texas Rangers won the American League pennant and the right to play the Cards in the World Series. For the third series in a row the Cardinals were underdogs. After winning game one, however, the Cardinals lost three of the next four games, winning only game three when Albert Pujols cracked three home runs. Entering game six in St. Louis, the Rangers needed only one more win to take the series. The Cardinals' magic appeared to have run out.

The Rangers were loose before the game, confident of victory and laughing and joking with one another on the field. Meanwhile, the Cardinals were worried. For the last six weeks they had told themselves to play one game, one inning, one pitch at a time, but now that they were facing the end of their season, that was a little more difficult to do.

With the score tied 4–4 entering the seventh inning, the Rangers erupted for three runs as both Nelson Cruz and Adrian Beltre hit home runs and Ian Kinsler knocked in another run with a single to make the score 7–4. In the Cardinals' dugout, the mood turned grim.

When the Cardinals came to bat in the bottom of the eighth, still trailing by three runs with only two innings remaining, the St. Louis crowd gave their team a half-hearted cheer. Although they appreciated what the Cardinals had done to reach the World Series, it was clear that their season was about to come to an end.

Then another player in the midst of a comeback stepped to the plate. His season should have ended two months earlier.

In June, Cardinals' outfielder Allen Craig had slid into a wall in Houston while chasing a fly ball. Hitting well over .300 at the time, he fractured his kneecap in the collision and was out of the lineup for the next two months. Most players with a fractured kneecap wouldn't have returned at all for the remainder of the season, and, in fact, after the World Series Craig would require surgery that would keep him from starting the 2012 season on time. But the Cardinals were fighting for the playoffs, and Craig was fighting to establish himself as a major leaguer. Although he couldn't run well, he could still play and had returned to the lineup in August. Thus far in the postseason he had managed to ignore the pain completely and in part-time duty had played well.

Craig had not been in the starting lineup, but Cardinals left fielder Matt Holliday had hurt a finger and in the seventh inning had to leave the game. Manager Tony LaRussa replaced him with Craig.

Even though Craig had started the game on the bench, his teammates had confidence in him. Although Craig was only a backup outfielder for the Cardinals, they told him that if he played on almost any other team in baseball, he would be a starting outfielder. Knowing his teammates had faith in him helped Craig stay ready.

Craig came to bat with one out in the bottom of the eighth against Rangers pitcher Derek Holland. In game four a few days before, Holland, a hard-throwing lefty who normally was a starting pitcher, had dominated the Cardinals, giving up only two hits and striking out seven for a 4–0 win. Allen Craig had faced Holland three times in that game and had struck out twice.

With a three-run lead, Holland went right after Craig with fastballs.

After one strike, Holland left a pitch over the plate and Craig swung as hard as he could. Maybe the Texas pitcher wasn't throwing quite as hard as he had in his last appearance, or perhaps Craig was just a little more focused, but this time instead of swinging through the pitch, a loud *crack!* echoed through the park as the bat met the ball.

It soared out to left field. Texas left fielder David Murphy drifted back, but the ball sailed over his head and into the stands for a home run, making the score 7–5.

The St. Louis crowd woke up and cheered raucously as Craig quickly ran around the bases. The Rangers were still in command, but now the Cardinals felt like they had a chance. As Lance Berkman said later, "Our attitude in the dugout was 'Why not?' Craig's hit was a critical play. All of a sudden you're only down two [runs] and two seems a lot closer than three, and the guys said, 'Let's make this interesting.'"

They did just that. After Holland got one more out, the Cardinals loaded the bases on three straight hits. Another base hit could tie the game. Cardinals fans were on their feet cheering wildly as shortstop Rafael Furcal came to the plate, but with his teammates ready to celebrate, Furcal grounded out. The cheers in the stands turned to groans, and the Rangers knew they were three outs away from becoming champions.

The Rangers went out quietly in the top of the ninth. As the Cardinals came to bat in the bottom of the inning, Texas manager Ron Washington put his closer, Neftali Feliz, into the game.

Feliz was one of the best closers in baseball. So far he had given up only one run in the postseason. During the regular season he had saved thirty-two games, and in the last few months had pitched particularly well. The chances of the Cardinals scoring even one run off Feliz were slim. In sixty-four appearances during the regular season, he had given up two or more runs only five times. Tying the game off Feliz — or winning — seemed almost impossible.

It became even less likely when Ryan Theriot, who led off the inning for the Cardinals, struck out. The Cardinals were two outs away from losing the game — and the series.

Big Albert Pujols came to bat next. He hadn't had a base hit in the World Series since hitting three home runs in game three. Feliz just focused on throwing strikes. He didn't want to put the tying run on base. Pujols, meanwhile, thought only about taking a good swing and making contact. A home run would be nice, but the Cardinals needed a base runner.

There was a reason Pujols had been selected as the National League's Most Valuable Player three times. He came through and ripped a pitch hard into the gap between left and center field.

Texas left fielder David Murphy and center fielder Josh Hamilton raced after the ball, but it skipped past them and rolled to the wall. Pujols, running cautiously, pulled up at second base with a double. Cardinals fans started to dream of a comeback.

So did the next hitter, Lance Berkman. "It's not fun to go up there with the season on the line," he later recalled. The base hit shook up Feliz, however, and he made it easy on Berkman, walking the hitter on four pitches and bringing Allen Craig, the potential winning run, to the plate. A home run would win the game, and a long extra-base hit could tie it. But at the same time, a double play could end the game. As a radio announcer said, "The next swing of the bat could win the game for the Cardinals, or could clinch the World Series for the Rangers." Or the game could continue.

After throwing two balls, Neftali Feliz settled down and rediscovered the strike zone, getting a called strike. With the fans in the stands pleading and praying for a base hit, Craig fouled off two pitches, and then left the bat on his shoulder as another pitch crossed the plate.

The umpire's arm shot up in the air. Strike three!

Craig slowly walked to the bench as David Freese stepped into the batter's box. Before his hometown crowd he would either be the hero or the last batter of the game.

He took a ball, then watched a strike pass.

The Rangers were poised to leap onto the field in celebration.

Feliz wound up and threw again. Another strike whistled toward the plate.

Freese swung and nearly fell to the ground as he missed the pitch. "He definitely blew that one by me," Freese said later.

Feliz and the Rangers were one strike away from victory, and Freese and the Cardinals one strike away from defeat. But Freese knew that in his career he had already overcome bigger odds than what he now faced. After all, what were the chances that a kid who quit baseball after high school would ever find himself playing in the big leagues, much less in the World Series with a chance to win the game? Besides, he had been coming through all year long. There was no reason he could not do so again.

Feliz got the sign from his catcher. Freese knew Feliz would try to blow another ball past him.

Feliz threw. The ball tailed out over the plate as Freese swung.

He hit the ball square and it rose on a line toward left field. As soon as he made contact both Pujols and Berkman started running as fast as they could.

Texas right fielder Nelson Cruz started running back. At first it looked as if he might catch up to the ball, but a leg injury made it difficult for him to run.

As Cruz approached the right field wall, he saw the ball coming down and jumped. Cardinals fans across the country held their breath.

The ball hit the wall just over Cruz's glove and bounced back toward the infield. Cruz awkwardly banged into the wall. Base hit!

Pujols raced around third and headed toward home. As he crossed the plate Lance Berkman, not known for speed, tore around third base as the Texas outfielder tracked down the ball. Berkman scored standing up and Freese dove headfirst into third for a triple. Tie ball game, 7–7! The Cardinals had come back!

Now they had a chance to win the game. A base hit would allow Freese to score. Catcher Bengie Molina stepped up to the plate. He hit the ball hard, but this time Nelson Cruz made the catch and the game went into extra innings.

Incredibly, improbably, implausibly, the Cardinals had tied the game. But the outcome was still up for grabs. The Cardinals had to score a run, and they had to stop Texas.

Now it was the Rangers' turn to bat. With one out in the top of the tenth, their shortstop, Elvis Andrus, singled off reliever Jason Motte. That brought outfielder Josh Hamilton to the plate.

Hamilton, who had been named the American League MVP after the 2010 season, had already completed quite a comeback of his own. Once considered one of the best prospects in the history of baseball, signing with the Tampa Bay Rays organization after graduating high school in 1999, Hamilton had lost his way. While playing in the minor leagues he began to abuse drugs, eventually becoming an addict. He was suspended several times and from 2004 until 2006 hardly played baseball at all, instead choosing to drink and use drugs.

Then Hamilton took control of his life. It wasn't easy, and he suffered a few relapses on the way, but he eventually overcame his addictions, worked his way back into shape, and resumed his baseball career. He became one of the best hitters in the game. So far, however, the Cardinals had held him in check during the World Series.

This time, however, Hamilton showed why he was so feared. He turned on a pitch and sent the ball deep into the stands in right field. The Rangers led again, 9–7.

There seemed no possible way St. Louis could come back from a two-run deficit for the second time in the same game. Doing so once had been a miracle. There wasn't even a word for doing it again.

But the team that had been coming back all season long did not know how to quit.

Daniel Delcalso led off the tenth with a soft ground ball to right that just made it through the infield for a base hit. Then pitcher Darren Oliver jammed hitter Jon Jay. He hit the ball off his fists down the left field line.

The ball floated over the head of third baseman Adrian Beltre into no man's land behind third base, then plunked to the ground just fair for another base hit. Kyle Lohse bunted Delcalso to third, but then Ryan Theriot grounded out. Delcalso scored on the play, but the Cardinals were again only one out away from defeat.

The Rangers took no chances with Albert Pujols and

walked him intentionally. The next player they had to face was Lance Berkman. A little more than a year earlier, the New York Yankees had decided to let Berkman go, and his career had looked as if it might be over. Now he was up to bat with the World Series on the line.

Berkman tried not to think about that. In fact, as he said later, "I thought about nothing." He just wanted to react to the pitch. Texas pitcher Scott Feldman pitched and Berkman swung.

He did not hit the ball hard, but he hit it to a good place. The soft line drive floated over the infield and landed for a base hit in short center field. Jon Jay raced home and scored.

The game was tied *again*, 9–9! The Cardinals were still alive and their fans were half out of their minds with excitement.

Allen Craig came up with a chance to win the game, but he grounded out to end the inning.

In the top of the eleventh, the Rangers put the winning run on base, but failed to score. If the Cardinals scored in the bottom of the inning they would win the game.

It was more than four and a half hours since the game had started. Players on both teams were exhausted, but they were prepared to play twenty innings if they had to.

For the sixth time that evening, local boy David Freese stepped to the plate, friends and family scattered throughout the stands. This time he faced Texas relief pitcher Mark Lowe. So far in the postseason Freese had played the best baseball of his life, leading all postseason hitters in RBIs. Cardinals fans hoped he would continue his hot hitting. They all believed in him.

Lowe threw one pitch. Freese swung, and time seemed to stop.

The ball rocketed off his bat far into the night, one bright spot against the darkness, rising as if held in the air by the hopes and dreams of Cardinals fans. Freese started running to first, looking at the ball in the sky, and as it began to drop down, he started to believe.

In center field, Josh Hamilton of the Rangers turned around and started to run, then slowed.

The ball dropped from the sky and onto the grass embankment beyond the center field fence.

Home run! Freese half ran and half jumped round the bases as his teammates gathered at home plate. As he rounded third, he grabbed his helmet from his head, threw it in the air in celebration, and jumped into the arms of his teammates, touching home plate and then disappearing in an enormous group hug.

The Cardinals — somehow, someway — had won, 10–9!

As Freese admitted later, "I've never been met at home plate by my team before." Never in his career, not even in Little League, had David Freese hit a walk-off home run.

And one night later, after the Rangers took a 2–0 first-inning lead off Chris Carpenter, Freese came through again, tying the game with a double. Then Allen Craig put the Cardinals ahead with a home run, and Lance Berkman chipped in with another hit, scoring another big run. Chris Carpenter shut down the Texas Rangers, and the Cardinals won game seven, 6–2 — making them World Champions and sending the Cardinals piling on top of one another in celebration once again.

It was an astounding victory, perhaps the greatest comeback in the history of sports. Even David Freese could hardly believe it, later saying, "I'm speechless, to be honest. When I sit down and think about winning this thing, I have yet to grasp what we, as a team, have accomplished."

Against all odds, by believing in each other, by never giving up, the Cardinals came back to win the most coveted championship — the World Series.

///

SOURCES AND FURTHER READING

When I write a book I use many different sources of information, including newspaper stories, interviews, magazine articles, books, video documentaries, and the Internet.

If you would like to learn more about any of the athletes discussed in this book, or others who have beaten the odds by never giving up, ask your teacher or school or town librarian for help. They may be able to show you how to find newspaper and magazine articles and other information online or lead you to some of the sources listed below, many of which were helpful to me when writing this book. The books may be purchased online or through any bookstore, or borrowed from your local library. And if your library does not have a copy, the librarian can probably borrow it for you from another library.

One of the best things about being a teacher or librarian is helping kids, so don't be shy about asking for help. And please keep reading!

TIM TEBOW

Through My Eyes by Tim Tebow and Nathan Whitaker (Harper, 2011). This book, written before the 2011 sea-

son, tells Tim's story through his first professional season and does a particularly good job of discussing his
high school and college career.

DenverBroncos.com
 The Broncos website has stories about every Broncos
 game during Tim Tebow's career.

"Mile High Power" by Damon Hack, *Sports Illustrated*, January 16, 2012.

"The Power of the Possible" by Jim Trotter, *Sports Illustrated*, December 9, 2012.

"Tim Tebow's Wild Ride" by Alan Shipnuck, *Sports Illustrated*, November 28, 2012.

There are many other newspaper and magazine articles
about Tim, and you can find video of some of his amazing
comebacks during the 2011 season on YouTube.

ROY RIEGELS

The Day Roy Riegels Ran the Wrong Way by Dan Gutman
 and Kerry Talbott (illustrator). Bloomsbury USA, 2011.
 Although written for younger children, this is the only
 book about Roy Riegels and his wrong-way run.

You can watch Roy's run on YouTube at www.youtube.
com/watch?v=dA8ShsySc48. Search "wrong-way run" on

YouTube to find videos of other players running the wrong way.

FRANK REICH

You can read more about Frank Reich and the Buffalo Bills' comeback in these two books:

Game Changers: The Greatest Plays in Buffalo Bills Football History by Marv Levy and Jeff Miller. Triumph Books, 2009.

Great Moments in Football History by Matt Christopher. Text by Glenn Stout. Little, Brown, 1997.

A YouTube video called "Greatest Comeback in NFL History" shows highlights of Frank Reich and the Bills' amazing victory over the Oilers: www.youtube.com/watch?v = piEHDtG1emU.

TRACY McGRADY

NBA Reader: Tracy McGrady by John Hareas. Scholastic, 2006.

See a video of Tracy's amazing performance, "Tracy McGrady: 13 points in 33 seconds," on YouTube at www.youtube.com/watch?v = ceLlz7dOOvY, and find many other sensational plays by Tracy.

2011 ST. LOUIS CARDINALS

The Year of the St. Louis Cardinals: Celebrating the 2011 World Series Champions, Official MLB Collector's Edition. Fenn-M&S, 2011.

APPENDIX

TIM TEBOW CAREER STATISTICS

FULL NAME: Timothy Richard Tebow

BORN: August 14, 1987, in Makati City, Philippines

HEIGHT: 6'3"   WEIGHT: 245 lbs.

POSITION: QB   COLLEGE: Florida

Drafted by the Denver Broncos in the 1st round (25th overall) of the 2010 NFL Draft.

		Passing							Rushing			
Season	Team	Att	Comp	Pct	Yds	TD	INT	Sack	Att	Yds	TD
COLLEGE											
2006	Florida Gators	33	22	66.7	358	5	1	0	89	469	8
2007	Florida Gators	350	234	66.9	3,286	32	6	13	210	895	23
2008	Florida Gators	298	192	64.4	2,747	30	4	15	176	673	12
2009	Florida Gators	304	213	70.1	2,895	21	5	25	217	910	14
	Totals	985	661	67.1	9,286	88	16	53	692	2,947	57
PROFESSIONAL											
2010	Denver	82	41	50.0	654	5	3	6	43	227	5
2011	Denver	271	126	46.5	1,729	12	6	33	122	660	6
	Totals	353	167	47.3	2,383	17	9	39	165	887	11

UNIVERSITY OF CALIFORNIA GOLDEN BEARS 1928 SEASON RECORD

Santa Clara	W	22–0
St. Mary's	W	7–0
Washington State	W	13–3
USC	T	0–0
Olympic Club	L	0–12
Washington	W	6–0
Nevada	W	60–0
Stanford	T	13–13
Georgia Tech	L	8–7 (Rose Bowl)
Final Record:	5–2–2	

FRANK REICH'S CAREER STATISTICS

Born: December 4, 1961, in Freeport, New York

Year	Team	Games	Starts	Comp	Att	Pct	Yds	Avg	TD	Int
1985	Buffalo Bills	1	—	1	1	100.0	19	19.0	0	0
1986	Buffalo Bills	3	—	9	19	47.4	104	5.5	0	2
1987	Buffalo Bills	0	—	—	—	—	—	—	—	—
1988	Buffalo Bills	3	—	—	—	—	—	—	—	—
1989	Buffalo Bills	7	—	53	87	60.9	701	8.1	7	2
1990	Buffalo Bills	16	—	36	63	57.1	469	7.4	2	0
1991	Buffalo Bills	16	1	27	41	65.9	305	7.4	6	2
1992	Buffalo Bills	16	0	24	47	51.1	221	4.7	0	2
1993	Buffalo Bills	15	0	16	26	61.5	153	5.9	2	0
1994	Buffalo Bills	16	2	56	93	60.2	568	6.1	1	4
1995	Carolina Panthers	3	3	37	84	44.0	441	5.3	2	2
1996	New York Jets	10	7	175	331	52.9	2,205	6.7	15	16
1997	Detroit Lions	6	0	11	30	36.7	121	4.0	0	2
1998	Detroit Lions	6	2	63	110	57.3	768	7.0	5	4
TOTAL				508	932	54.5	6,075	6.5	40	36

TRACY McGRADY'S CAREER STATISTICS

BORN: May 24, 1979, in Bartow, Florida

Year	Team	Games	Field goal %	Three point %	Free throw %	Points
1997–98	Toronto	64	45.0	34.2	71.2	7.1
1998–99	Toronto	49	43.6	22.9	72.6	9.4
1999–00	Toronto	79	45.1	27.7	70.7	15.4
2000–01	Orlando	77	45.7	35.5	73.3	26.8
2001–02	Orlando	76	45.1	36.4	74.8	25.6
2002–03	Orlando	75	45.7	38.6	79.3	32.1
2003–04	Orlando	67	41.7	33.9	79.6	28.0
2004–05	Houston	78	43.1	32.6	77.4	25.7
2005–06	Houston	47	40.6	31.2	74.7	24.4
2006–07	Houston	71	43.1	33.1	70.7	24.6
2007–08	Houston	66	41.9	29.2	68.4	21.6
2008–09	Houston	35	38.8	37.6	80.1	15.6
2009–10	Houston	6	36.8	50.0	66.7	3.2
2009–10	New York	24	38.9	24.2	75.4	9.4
2010–11	Detroit	72	44.2	34.1	69.8	8.0
TOTAL		**886**	**43.5**	**33.7**	**74.7**	**20.4**

ST. LOUIS CARDINALS 2011 POSTSEASON RECORD

National League Division Series					STL	PHI
Game 1	STL	@	PHI	L	6	11
Game 2	STL	@	PHI	W	5	4
Game 3	STL		PHI	L	2	3
Game 4	STL		PHI	W	5	3
Game 5	STL	@	PHI	W	1	0
Cardinals win 3–2						
National League Championship Series					STL	MIL
Game 1	STL	@	MIL	L	6	9
Game 2	STL	@	MIL	W	12	3
Game 3	STL		MIL	W	4	3
Game 4	STL		MIL	L	2	4
Game 5	STL		MIL	W	7	1
Game 6	STL	@	MIL	W	12	6
Cardinals win 4–2						
World Series					STL	TEX
WS Game 1	STL		TEX	W	3	2
WS Game 2	STL		TEX	L	1	2
WS Game 3	STL	@	TEX	W	16	7
WS Game 4	STL	@	TEX	L	0	4
WS Game 5	STL	@	TEX	L	2	4
WS Game 6	STL		TEX	W	10	9
WS Game 7	STL		TEX	W	6	2
Cardinals win 4–3						

GOOD·SPORTS
BY GLENN STOUT

PLAYING FOR THE LOVE OF THE GAME!

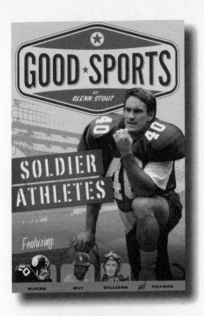

GOOD★SPORTS
BY GLENN STOUT

SOLDIER
ATHLETES

Featuring:

BLEIER   MAY   WILLIAMS *and* TILLMAN

GOOD★SPORTS
BY GLENN STOUT

ABLE TO
PLAY

Featuring:

BROWN   ABBOTT   SANTO   PRIDE

GOOD★SPORTS
BY GLENN STOUT

AGAINST
ALL
ODDS

Featuring:

TEBOW

HEIGELS   2011 CARDINALS   REICH *and* MCGRADY

GOOD★SPORTS
BY GLENN STOUT

FROM
HARDSHIPS TO
CHAMPIONSHIPS

Featuring:

HUNTER   PIERSALL   TORRE   LeFLORE *and* RUTH

FACT OR FICTION? READ THESE AWESOME NOVELS ABOUT SPORTS AND ATHLETES.

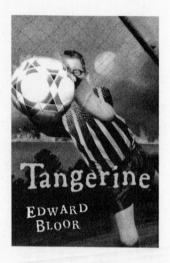

PEAK

The emotional, tension-filled story of a fourteen-year-old boy's attempt to be the youngest person to reach the top of Mount Everest.

TANGERINE

In Tangerine County, Florida, weird is normal. Lightning strikes at the same time every day, a sinkhole swallows a local school, and Paul the geek finds himself adopted into the toughest group around: the middle school soccer team.

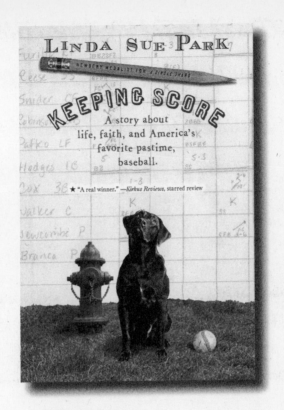

KEEPING SCORE

Nine-year-old Maggie learns a lot about baseball and life in this historical novel set during the Korean War and the Dodgers' 1951 season.

FIND MORE FUN AND FUNNY
BIOGRAPHIES IN THE LIVES
OF . . . SERIES BY KATHLEEN KRULL,
ILLUSTRATED BY KATHRYN HEWITT:

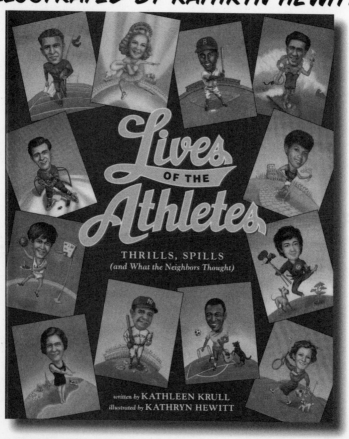

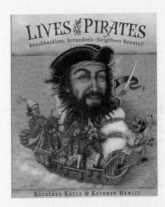

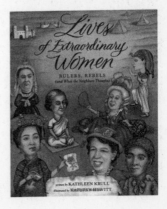

ABOUT THE AUTHOR

When Glenn Stout was growing up outside a small town in central Ohio, he never dreamed that he would become a writer. Then reading changed his life. As a kid, Glenn played baseball, basketball, and football, but baseball was always his favorite sport. Glenn studied poetry and creative writing in college and has had many different jobs, including selling minor league baseball tickets, cleaning offices, grading papers for a college, and painting houses. He also worked as a construction worker and a librarian. Glenn started writing professionally while he was working at the Boston Public Library and has been a full-time writer since 1993. Under the auspices of Matt Christopher, Glenn wrote forty titles in the Matt Christopher sports biography series, and every year he edits *The Best American Sports Writing* collection. Some of Glenn's other books include *Red Sox Century*, *Yankees Century*, *Nine Months at Ground Zero*, and *Young Woman and the Sea: How Trudy Ederle Conquered the English Channel and Inspired the World*. He has written or edited more than seventy books.

Glenn is a citizen of both the United States and Canada and lives on Lake Champlain in Vermont with his wife, daughter, one cat, one dog, and a rabbit. He writes in a messy office in his basement, and when he isn't working, he likes to ski, skate, hike in the woods, kayak on the lake, take photographs, and read.